I would like to thank David Wilkerson for
giving me the freedom to tell this story as
I saw it; Joseph Tarallo, associate art director
of *Look*, for his many hours of work in
designing this book; and writers Kay Nelson
and Steve Singer, and photographers Douglas
Gilbert and W. Eugene Smith for their
encouragement and suggestions.

Bob Combs

GOD'S TURF

FLEMING H. REVELL COMPANY, OLD TAPPAN, NEW JERSEY

GOD'S TURF

BOB COMBS

Acknowledgment is made for material by the Rev. Norman C. Eddy in "The Clergyman's Viewpoint," from *Problems in Addiction: Alcohol and Drug Addiction*, ed. William C. Bier, S.J. (New York: Fordham University Press, 1962), pp. 203-207.

TO MY MOTHER.

CONTENTS

INTRODUCTION

In the ten years since Teen Challenge was founded, more than one-half million words have been published about its ministries, about those it serves, and about the observations and knowledge gained through serving. There are times, however, when even the most carefully chosen words seem inadequate.

It is difficult to describe the absolute degradation of a drug addict as he mutilates his body with a needle.

It is hard to create a word-picture of the tortured existence of a ghetto child, living in the midst of misery, addiction and violence, or the haunting loneliness of a teen-age girl who has turned to prostitution to support her own or her boyfriend's habit.

About two years ago, a rather serious, intense young man was shown into my office. Bob Combs introduced himself as a magazine photographer acquiring a master's degree in journalism at Boston University. "I have read *The Cross and the Switchblade* with great interest," he said, "and that is a story that should be told photographically. Most photo-journalists are not concerned with Christianity, or religion, but I feel very different. I am anxious to show what God is doing here." That very week I had been looking at a picture book and thinking how wonderful it would be if something like it could be done on the work of Teen Challenge!

The following summer Bob joined our staff. He arrived with an old car, a few clothes, his cameras and a Christ-inspired desire to contribute his particular talents. As he became familiar with the programs — the counseling, the farms and girls' home, the evangelistic teams — his contributions were clearly evident. Our monthly publication, album covers, pamphlets and booklets improved graphically because of his skills, but for the past eighteen months his overriding goal has been the completion of this photographic essay.

Turf is a currently popular slang term meaning one's own neighborhood or street, and in some of the poorest, most sin-ridden neighborhoods imaginable, God is performing miracles every day. The evidences of His love are dramatically present. There are photographs in this book that will make the most hardened wince, but there are others that will evoke rejoicing. The following pages provide a tour of *God's Turf* as seen through the camera lens of Bob Combs. Misery and miracles, low life and new life — see it like it is.

David Wilkerson

THE WALKING DEAD

To be a confirmed drug addict is to be one of the walking dead.
— New York City Police Department

For walking corpses they moved very lively that bright, fall afternoon. The two jaywalked across Lexington Avenue nimbly dodging the traffic. Heading east, they walked intently along East 107th Street past clusters of people sitting and chatting on tenement steps and garbage cans.

The rhythm of their steps was interrupted neither by the many children playing on the sidewalk nor by a friend who smirked and said, "Luis. Carlos. *¿Qué pasa?* [What's happening?]."

Something was going to happen, but the two were not about to discuss it. They didn't have to. No answer was necessary. Even the children playing hopscotch and spinning tops on the sidewalk knew what their quick, nervous steps and determined expressions meant.

The pair turned into a narrow passageway between two tenements and stopped in front of a basement door. It stuck. They kicked it open. Immediately were greeted by a torrent of profanity.

"You damned junkies. Get outta here or I call the cops."

Confronting them was a wino so filthy it was impossible to distinguish his skin color. The junkies pushed through and chained the door to keep out sober intruders — especially those in uniform — while the wino cursed them with a fury.

Another drunk appeared. The long, raggle-taggle hair suggested a woman. "Don't bother them," she pleaded. "They'll hurt you."

The wino snarled at her, but the woman produced a half-empty bottle, and he willingly followed her to another section of the basement without further comment.

Luis immediately began probing a crevice behind several water pipes. Carlos rummaged through a pile of old boards in a corner, sneezing once at the dust. Each found a little package wrapped in brown paper. Luis filled a grimy Pepsi bottle with water from a rusty, cobweb-covered pipe.

The two sat tensely on orange crates, unwrapping their "works": an eyedropper topped with a pacifier nipple, a hypodermic needle and a blackened bottle cap. "Spikes," as the needles are called, were placed on the eyedroppers and "cleaned" with water from the bottle.

Luis slit open several postage-stamp-size glassine envelopes and dumped the white, powdery heroin into the bottlecap cooker. To this he added a *bombita,* a vial of liquid stimulant purchased from the pusher. This liquid pep pill allows the heroin user to function almost normally instead of nodding drowsily for several hours.

Perspiration trickled down both faces while a match flame danced under the blackened cooker for several seconds to dissolve the heroin. They wrapped belts tightly around their arms, then drew the liquid into the needles through a dab of cotton meant to filter impurities. The two flexed their arms several times. Veins, some purple and discolored, protruded. Luis immediately "hit" a surface vein. He had been "shooting" heroin

"Once you put the spike in your arm,
that's it. I ain't never seen a
dude who took a shot and stopped."

for only two years.

Because Carlos had been addicted somewhat longer, many of his surface veins had collapsed. He moved his needle back and forth under the skin until he located a vein. Then he squeezed the pacifier nipple and released it. The heroin made a round trip into the vein and back to the needle. He booted, as they call it, several more times for an extra kick, and injected the heroin when blood began to coat the inside of the eyedropper.

Both sighed with relief. Lighting cigarettes, they sat peacefully for a minute and then, after rinsing and rewrapping their works, stashed them in new hiding places. The danger of discovery and arrest past, the two sat on the steps outside and "rapped." Tension and nervousness had passed — temporarily. Soon they would need another fix.

Each day in New York City this process is repeated thousands of times on rooftops, in apartments, on stairways, in bathrooms and in other basements. Carlos and Luis are but two of thousands of heroin addicts.

No one is certain of the exact number. There are over 60,000 known heroin addicts in the United States, half of them in New York City. Dr. Efren Ramirez, who formerly co-ordinated New York City's programs on addiction, estimates that there are over 100,000 addicts in this city alone. A few believe that those addicted to morphine, heroin and related drugs in the United States could number as high as 1,000,000.

Astounding as the estimates are, narcotics addiction is not a new problem in the United States. "I did not, I could not conceive the

The moment of truth for two addicts in Spanish Harlem. Carlos searches for a functioning vein in his arm with his spike, while Luis mixes his heroin with bombita, *a stimulant.*

mental hell into whose fierce corroding fires I was about to enter" is not the confession of a forlorn addict of the 1960's. It was written by a young immigrant in 1842 after he became addicted to opium.

In the nineteenth century, opium was smoked by the Chinese, eaten by many business and professional people, and prescribed for countless ailments by doctors who did not understand the danger of the drug. Morphine, an opium-based drug, was widely used as a pain-killer during the Civil War. So many soldiers returned home addicted that their condition was referred to as the "soldier's illness." At that time, patent medicines and some soft drinks containing opium could be bought legally in almost any store. Even heroin was thought to be non-addictive when it was introduced in 1898 as a treatment for morphine addiction. The net result was that by 1910 there were between 200,000 and 1,000,000 narcotic addicts in the United States. One person in 400 was thought to be addicted to narcotics in some form. Today, the estimate is one in 3,500.

Federal controls and legislation (especially the Harrison Act in 1914) eliminated legal narcotics sources and did much to curb the

rising addiction rate. For their supply, addicts turned to the underworld, which obligingly met the demand — for a very high price.

Today, the underworld has turned the illegal narcotics trade into its most lucrative operation. Ten kilos of opium (22 pounds) purchased from a poppy farmer in Turkey for $350 will make, after refinement, sixteen kilos of five percent heroin which will sell for over $400,000 on the streets of New York. There, pure heroin is worth over 250 times as much as gold.

The heroin an addict injects may originate in Red China or the Far East, where in some

The "works" (the needle-tipped eyedropper and the bottle-cap "cooker") are stashed immediately because their possession is illegal. Then the two sit and rap on garbage-strewn tenement steps. Having injected bombita with their heroin, they are able to function almost normally — while high.

weeks in 1967 more Asians were killed fighting for the control of opium than were killed on the battlefields of Vietnam. It may come from illicit poppy fields in Mexico, but more likely, the heroin began its furtive trek in Turkey as opium. Enroute to Marseilles, France, the heart of the international drug traffic, it will be converted from opium to morphine, perhaps in Syria or Lebanon. Once in Marseilles, it will again be converted, this time into heroin.

It arrives in New York in one of many ingenious ways, or perhaps more simply, in one of the innumerable hiding places in a passenger ship or freighter. Eventually it reaches the junkie through a channel of distributors, many of whom are Negro and Puerto Rican, unseen and untouched by the Mafia chieftain who ordered it. Although the Mafia has controlled illegal narcotic traffic in the United States for years, Cuban gangsters are reported to be moving in.

What compels heroin addicts and abusers (those not yet addicted) to pay such inflated prices for this narcotic? Psychiatrists say that many users are seeking relief from their anxieties.

John, a twenty-nine-year-old addict, put it

vides a kick. Probably most addicts begin using heroin for this reason — kicks.

Teen-agers are especially susceptible. In the late 1950's and early 60's, the members of New York's fighting gangs discovered a bigger kick than "sneaky pete," a cheap wine that sneaks up and hits you when you don't expect it. A young teen-ager would prove himself to be one of the boys by both downing a drink and smoking a marijuana cigarette.

Soon, instead of, "Have a joint," his friends would say, "Take a snort. C'mon, whasa madda. You chicken?" Not likely. So he would sniff heroin.

A bigger kick is "skin-popping," injecting heroin in skin tissue. "Kids snort. Men use spikes." So the argument goes.

The largest charge is "mainlining" — "drilling" a vein. For the heroin user, this is the ultimate kick — and the ultimate step down the road to addiction.

Heroin is no longer confined only to shook-up kids, the delinquents. When one Bedford-Stuyvesant (Brooklyn) teen-ager told me, "Half the kids I know have tried heroin," he probably wasn't exaggerating. One four-year study conducted on a single block in Spanish Harlem revealed that one-third of the teen-agers became heroin addicts during that time. Many of the others probably tried it once or twice.

To meet the demand, a few pushers offer student-size "deuce" (two dollar) bags in addition to the usual "treys" (three dollar) and "nickle" bags (five dollars). These prices vary in different areas.

No teen-ager, in fact, no heroin user, expects to become addicted. If he lives in the slums he probably knows addicts and junkies, but *he's* too smart, too tough, to end up like them. *He'll* never be the slob who, when he's out of jail and not looking for something to steal, sits on tenement steps either dozing under the influence of heroin, itching because the heroin was cut with quinine, or writhing in withdrawal pain. Not *him.*

His first experience with heroin proves he's right. No withdrawal symptoms. *He's* tough. So he tries it again. And again. If he remains a weekend user, a "joy-popper," he will not become addicted, but the temptation is almost overwhelming to shoot more and more

more simply. "I've been on the stuff since I was sixteen. Why? I'll tell you the God-honest truth. Most guys start because they are afraid. I did.

"There are lots of kinds of fear, not just the kind you'd have if someone with a gun chased you down the street. Fear of a job, fear of responsibility, fear of facing people: these are some.

"When you shoot up you forget all this. When you're high you don't think about nothin'. Everything's cool. Beautiful."

Because heroin is a drug of escape, it should come as no surprise that heroin users usually live in slums where there is the most to escape from: poor housing, little food, broken homes, lack of opportunity, and endless dirt and garbage. About seventy percent

---

"Drugs are like marriage — great at first, then when the thrill wears off, you're trapped."

Twenty-nine-year-old married addict.

---

of the users in New York City are Negroes, Puerto Ricans, and Mexicans; they live in the worst slum areas.

Not all addicts are hopeless outcasts seeking oblivion. Well-known musicians and entertainers, a sports announcer whose name was a household word, and at least one important member of Congress are or have been addicted. Hundreds of doctors and nurses are addicted to morphine. Perhaps these sought in heroin and morphine a source of inner security and a relief from tension and pain.

For the unwary thrill-seeker, heroin pro-

often. One day he runs short of money, and he misses his fix. To his amazement he is restless, his nose runs, his whole body aches, and he vomits.

He's hooked! His intoxicating friend has become his brutal master. What began as a game is now to him a life and death struggle. Drugs become all important. Girls, food, and what others think of him matter less and less.

His body has built a tolerance to heroin. Without it, the chemical balance of billions of blood cells is changed and withdrawal begins. Also because of this tolerance, he no longer gets the kick he first got from heroin. The honeymoon is over — unless he shoots more and more.

Perhaps he works to buy the ever-increasing quantity he needs to get high, but almost inevitably he loses his job. He then pawns everything of value he owns or can steal. When his family discovers his plight, he will probably be thrown out so he won't lead his brothers and sisters astray.

"I've seen death nine times. One of these times I was in the bathroom of a barber shop. The owner noticed that I took a real long time, and when he came to check there was water running out from under the door. I was laying flat on my back, out cold.

"He helped me out. I was so embarrassed. The place was filled with kids and older men and I was a mess. He could have turned me in — my works were in the sink — but he didn't."

Addict who took an overdose.

Usually an addict's parents and relatives are among his first victims. One mother, seeing her furniture and possessions disappear piece by piece, temporarily evicted her addicted teen-age son. She withdrew her savings from the bank and invested the several hundred dollars in burglar-proof locks. Then she gave her son only the key to the hallway door to his room. She lived barricaded in the adjoining rooms with what furniture she was able to rescue from local pawnshops.

Most addicts turn to shoplifting, burglary and other crimes involving property. They steal an estimated one billion dollars worth of goods each year to support their habits.

Because the goods are "hot" they get far less than the merchandise is worth, usually only one-tenth to one-fifth the actual value.

Eventually the addict is arrested. Jail seldom rehabilitates him. As soon as he is released he returns to his spike, probably better equipped to buy or steal drugs because of his confinement in a crime school.

Aaron Johnson, once an addict, said, "The older convicts and the older addicts sit around in groups and talk about various ways of stealing, who to see about buying a large quantity of drugs, who's the largest dealer and things like that."

An addict can be sent up for stealing purses and come out knowing how to forge checks, how to burglarize a drugstore for narcotics, how to pick a pocket, how to use a variety of con games, how to break into cars without being seen, how to hot-line (steal) an automobile and where to sell it.

Whether male or female, and addict will probably push heroin at one time or another. The penalty for dealing is more severe than for possession, but there are advantages. Pushing is profitable and the addict always has a ready supply of dope.

However, easy access does not keep his body from developing a tolerance to the drug. For forty or fifty dollars each day he might function normally, but still not get high. If he has been a long-time user, he might shoot "speedballs" (heroin plus cocaine), or supplement his "H" with pills to recapture the original exhilaration. Heroin addicts shun violence and crimes of violence, but not "pillheads." Both barbiturates and amphetamines, if taken to excess, can lead to paranoid and often violent behavior. And barbiturate withdrawal is more of a catastrophe than heroin withdrawal.

As an addict increases his dosage his chances of taking an overdose ("O.D.") increase. However, that possibility is always present. A heroin user can never tell how strong his stuff is before he injects it. It may be nothing but milk, sugar and quinine. It may be a normal three to ten percent amount of heroin or a fatal seventy percent.

When he injects more heroin than his body can tolerate the addict becomes unconscious, possibly before he can remove the needle. Perhaps he will recover; perhaps he will die.

If a friend is present, his friend might shake him, slap him, inject salt water into a vein or leave in a panic, afraid to be discovered with a dead man. Although it isn't always fatal, O.D. is a major cause of death among youth in New York City.

At one time pushers gave nearly pure heroin to troublesome customers and to "rats" (suspected police informers). Today, rats are sold rat poison or lye. Both are as fatal as heroin and more economical.

In addition to being vulnerable to O.D., the heroin user is a candidate for malnutrition for while on heroin he loses interest in food. Because of unsterilized needles, the user is susceptible to hepatitis and lockjaw. About three-fourths of the lockjaw cases in New York City are narcotics addicts.

Marijuana, the beginning of the end for many.

Sooner or later an addict is likely to admit himself into a hospital to kick his habit. Perhaps he wants a cure, but more likely he wants to cut his habit back to a level he can afford. He also wants to regain his health. If there were no jails or hospitals for addicts to recuperate in, most addicts would probably die.

Even among those who want help, few are actually cured at hospitals that treat addicts. An addict who was waiting to buy heroin on a cold, windy street corner in the Bronx told me, "Your friend mentioned Manhattan General [Hospital]. I've been there and to other hospitals, too. They 'cure' you all right. They build you up and send you out — to start all over again.

"Man, it's up here, in your mind. They can help you kick physically but that's not the hang-up.

"When you're there you think beautiful thoughts. You say, 'Man, what am I doing here? Never again. This time I'll stay clean.'

"But when you get out you see that people are still the same and you go right back."

So many addicts returned to heroin after leaving the Riverside Hospital that the hospital reported, when it closed its doors: "Any organized program dealing with the problem of drug addiction is faced with the historical fact that no therapeutic success of any significance has ever been recorded."

The U.S. Public Health Hospital in Lexington Kentucky, has not been significantly successful either. Less than one in ten of its former patients say "clean," free fom heroin.

Synanon is perhaps the best-known private drug rehabilitation program. As soon as they are admitted, its addicts — probably more highly motivated and better educated than most — begin to learn about themselves primarily through group therapy sessions, which often become gutter-rough.

Synanon is successful in that the hundreds of addicts *on the premises* are voluntarily off drugs; but in terms of curing addicts and returning them clean to society, Synanon is not successful, according to the chairman of

"Using drugs is a duel with the devil. You're messin' with the depths of hell."

A junkie's home in a fire-gutted tenement.

the New York State Council on Drug Addiction. In eight years over 1,200 addicts entered Synanon voluntarily. Only seventy returned clean to the community.

Synanon, Daytop Village, Exodus House, Narcotics Anonymous and dozens of other programs are to be commended for trying, and in a few cases for succeeding in rehabilitating addicts and returning them to society as useful citizens. But most addicts are never exposed to rehabilitation programs, much less cured.

Methadone was heralded as a very suc-

cessful treatment for addiction. An addict enrolled in this state-sponsored program is hospitalized and given methadone as a substitute drug. After he is released he returns to the hospital periodically for his fix. I spoke to several addicts who tried methadone. They said they could not sleep while using it so they returned to heroin to get some rest. Other users have complained of hallucinations. In one two-year experiment no methadone user had withdrawn and returned to society drug-free. They remained hooked.

A few addicts have been able to kick physically, but then they have turned to large quantities of liquor, pills, or marijuana to satisfy their inner needs. Like most methadone users, they are still hooked.

Ten years ago, when someone suggested to an addict that he should seek help, he would scornfully say, "Once you're a junkie you're always a junkie." Since then, the quest for THE cure has been responsible for thousands of newspaper and magazine articles, dozens of new rehabilitation programs, committees, conferences and medical research. But many addicts still believe, "Once a junkie, always a junkie."

I
AM
A NUMBER

time
measured by an empty room
between heartbeats and paper prayers
or through a dusty window
the light seen
kissing particles and sliding down the wall
to trip over a picture
of trees and grass
and fall sprawling across the bones of a wooden chair
splashing the floor with forgotten warmth
and surprising the roaches playing king
on yesterday's paper
and finally creeping across the dresser
to bathe in a glass of bloody water
next to an eyedropper
and needle
two glassine bags
torn and empty
and the bottle top
still containing traces of yesterday's hope
there is no more
the door is locked
the bed is cold
and I am a number

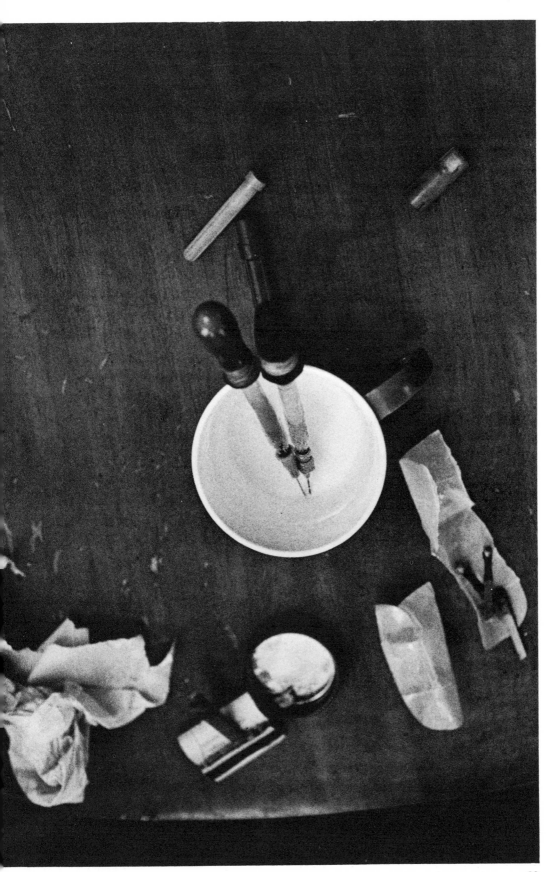

BROOKLYN

During the early 1960's the word got around. Addicts were being cured at Teen Challenge, a religious-oriented rehabilitation center in Brooklyn, New York. *Life* magazine called it a "worthy, highly successful approach." This magazine was itself indirectly responsible for the establishment of Teen Challenge.

One night in 1958 Rev. David Wilkerson, then a twenty-seven-year-old country pastor, opened a copy of *Life*. There he saw the desperate faces of seven teen-age gang members who had been indicted for the murder of a young cripple. Suddenly he knew he must help them. He had to go to New York.

Once arrived, he attended the murder trial. When the court adjourned, he approached the judge for permission to see the boys. Because of threats made against the judge's life during the trial, the guards were nervous, and David was immediately seized and searched. Though of course no weapon was found concealed on his person or in his Bible, Dave was evicted.

He wept in shame. By the time he returned home to Phillipsburg, Pennsylvania, his family and parishioners had already seen his picture in the newspaper with the headline, *Bible-waving Preacher Interrupts Murder Trial.*

This fiasco turned out to be a blessing in disguise, however. When later he began commuting to New York one day a week to work with the street gangs, he found that the boys regarded him a hero.

At a time when conditions were such that one journalist charged: "No one cares whether Bedford-Stuyvesant lives with God or the devil," David Wilkerson was walking its streets, talking to gang members and

"... For whatever the other professionals and fields of human endeavor may say about the problem, addiction to heroin is a symptom of deep rooted spiritual sickness, and a diabolical answer to the spiritual quest of the man without faith in God."

Rev. Norman Eddy, former Chairman of the New York Council on Narcotics Addiction.

sleeping in his car at night, obviously unknown to the journalist. And he was getting results.

When Dave first preached on a Brooklyn street corner, the two leaders of the notorious Chaplain gang knelt beside the curb to pray. Several months later Nicky Cruz, sadistic vice-president of the Mau Maus, decided to turn his life over to God.

Encouraged, and with little money but much faith, Dave quit his pastorate and moved to New York with his wife and two children. In the days that followed, Rebels, Chaplains, Mau Maus, Dragons, G.G.I's (Grand Gangsters Incorporated), Hellburners, and Roman Lords responded to his simple message: "God loves you. He'll change your life if you'll let Him."

Dave's dream of a house in which these

kids could be surrounded by love instead of hate and fear was answered in 1960. A stately Georgian building on Brooklyn's once-respectable Clinton Avenue was purchased.

From the time the first building was purchased, drug addicts had been admitted. Most were gang members. The gangs were slowly disintegrating because more and more teens were too busy hustling for money to buy heroin to bother rumbling. The teen addicts who wanted help could find little. Medical authorities tended to agree with the older addicts, "There's no hope for a junkie." But the word began to spread. "Teen Challenge has the answer." David Wilkerson's advice to gang members was working for addicts, too.

Today Teen Challenge has five buildings in Brooklyn, including a $400,000 spiritual therapy clinic. There is also a farm in Pennsylvania for spiritual and vocational rehabilitation, a home for troubled girls in Garrison, New York, an Institute of Missions to train Christian workers, and a counseling center in Greenwich Village. Across the nation and in several foreign countries there are twenty-eight other independent Teen Challenge centers.

Today, scores of converted drug addicts staff many Teen Challenge centers, hold responsible jobs and pastor churches. In Los Angeles, a former $100-a-day user pastors an all-junkie church in which the choir members and even the treasurer are former addicts.

The testimony of former addicts brings many of their addicted friends into a center. As one boy said, "I figured if it worked for him, it'd work for me. He used to be in a lot worse shape than me." Converted addicts also testify to God's power at street meetings held in heroin-infested neighborhoods. After testimonies, singing and preaching Teen Challenge workers mingle with addicts to tell them there is hope. The workers also pass out Teen Challenge literature. As many as forty addicts have come into the program as a result of a single street meeting.

Not all come at once, however. Most addicts won't give up heroin without a reason, but many keep the Teen Challenge booklet, *A Positive Cure for Drug Addiction,* in case of an emergency. It may be months and even years before they are led to seek help. For one boy, it was his frenzied mother. Watching her son gradually deteriorate was more than she could bear. She told him she would become a prostitute to help support his habit.

For some it is a flirt with death. One addict who was trying to break into an apartment missed a jump between fire escapes and fell five stories. Miraculously, his descent was slowed by numerous clotheslines, and he escaped with only a few broken bones. He decided to give up heroin while he was still alive.

Others come into the program after taking near-fatal overdoses. Some seek refuge from the police or from victims who are trying to get even. A few addicts desperately want help, but for many, Teen Challenge is merely a warm bed, three good meals, and a chance to regain strength. The latter have no intention of staying long.

No medication is given during withdrawal. However, "cold turkey" is not as painful as it was when the heroin sold on the street was

Many New York City addicts hear
of Teen Challenge from friends
who have been helped there or at
street meetings held in drug-
infested areas. Here, as a prostitute looks on, Aaron Johnson
(facing camera) tells one of his
former heroin customers of his
new life. Aaron, once an addict,
pimp and pusher, several months
later became the president of
his class at a Canadian Bible
school where he is studying for
the ministry.

An addict listens at a Teen Challenge meeting in Brooklyn.

"God can change your life too,"
says Rev. Victor Torres to
enemies he once shot at as a
member of the Roman Lords gang,
and to friends he "shot up"
with later as a junkie. Together with his wife, Victor
recently went to Argentina to
establish a Teen Challenge center.

purer, but it still is very unpleasant. Cold sweats, chills, restlessness, nausea, various aches and pains, and an almost overwhelming desire for heroin cause the freeloaders to leave in short order. It isn't surprising then that fifty percent leave during the first three days. Those who do stay find their withdrawal period is surprisingly short — less than the usual two weeks.

Another surprise comes when they begin to attend the daily chapel services and the Bible classes. Each weekday morning there is a chapel service; almost every afternoon there are prayer sessions and Bible classes; and every evening there is either a service or Bible class. The newcomer's reaction is usually, "They must be nuts!" Then he puts his sixth sense to work on the staff. To survive on the street, addicts must be able to size up people accurately and quickly. If they don't, they may be arrested or perhaps killed. Newcomers aren't about to be taken in by a bunch of religious fanatics, so they sit back and watch. One counselor said, "For the first few days they literally sit and stare at us. They try to figure out what we're like and how they can 'con' us and 'work angles.'" One group scrutinized and sometimes intentionally aggravated the staff for at least two months. They all confided later that the one thing that impressed them about the program was the genuine spiritual commitment of the counselors. As one said, "They're for real. They love God — and us, too."

The newcomer continually hears about the love of God, His forgiveness, and His power to rehabilitate spiritually, physically and mentally. To an addict who has been rejected by both society and his family, the assurance that someone loves him meets a real need. Before, he tried to rationalize his crimes by telling himself, "I couldn't help it. Heroin makes me do it." Yet, he is plagued with guilt. This makes the possibility of being forgiven especially inviting.

Once he decides to respond, perhaps many others will be affected as a result. Although Isaac Cordero came to the center with a bad attitude and a chip on his shoulder, he soon experienced God's forgiveness and love. This wasn't a sudden crisis, though; it was a gradual change. After two months he brought his brother to Teen Challenge.

The first Teen Challenge building at 416 Clinton Ave.

The new center at 444 Clinton Ave.

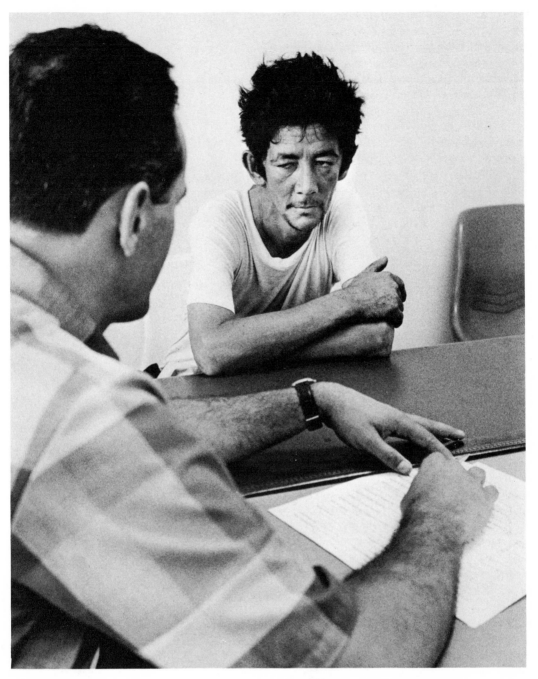

An interview with a counselor is the first stage of induction.
Many come ''strung out'' — weak and unkempt.

Thirty-five days and thirty pounds later.

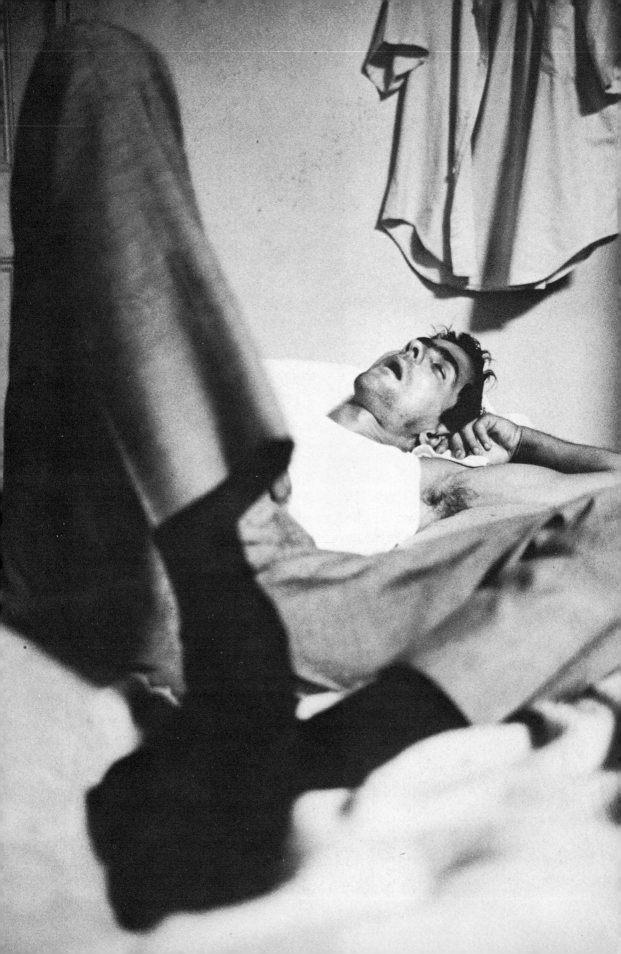

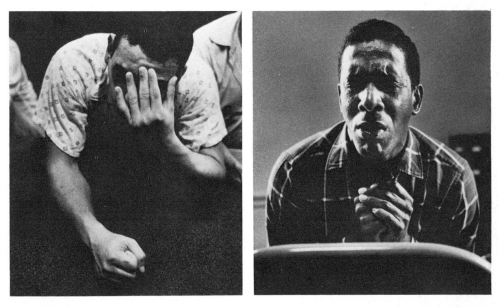

After withdrawal (left), each is encouraged to pray for help. Spiritual therapy is stressed.

Their enthusiasm grew by leaps and bounds. When they went home on a weekend pass they persuaded a half-dozen addicted friends to come back with them. One, convinced that he was "really onto something good," quit his $160-a-week job to kick his habit. The two brothers brought a third to a Saturday evening rally and he, too, accepted Christ. As soon as a fourth brother, Alex, was released from jail, he came to Teen Challenge. He later told a counselor, "When I was out on the streets, I was always where the action was. Man, I couldn't miss out on this."

This chain reaction began with one conversion experience, the first step in the spiritual therapy program. The men learn that this experience includes a "total cure for the total man," that is, freedom not only from heroin, but also alcohol, promiscuous sex, cursing and lying. Regardless of their religious background (about ninety percent are at least nominal Catholics — the rest are Protestant and Jewish), all are encouraged to pray for forgiveness, and to ask God to come into their lives. Even if a boy is at Teen Challenge only one day, he is almost certain to hear this verse, "Therefore if any man be in Christ, he is a new creature: old things are passed away; behold, all things are become new" (II Corinthians 5:17).

At the heart of the rehabilitation program is the conversion experience. It is also the target for much of the criticism leveled at Teen Challenge. Many professionals say it is only a "shallow emotional experience," but famous psychologist William James thought differently. He said that the results of Christian conversion are happiness, relaxation from tension, and the complete absence of

Chapel: sermons, songs and testimonies. One boy tells Rev. David Wilkerson and newcomers in the program what God has done for him.

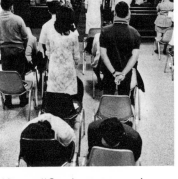

*Above: "On drugs me and my
brother were always together —
in basements and on rooftops.
Thank God we're both here."
Below: Saturday night rally.*

*A lively Spanish chorus
learned in chapel
is sung in the dorm.*

Robert M. shares a problem
with a counselor. After his
25th LSD trip, he took heroin
to relax and became hooked.

"A psychiatrist told me I'd
always be hooked on something,
so I should smoke a lot of
pot or drink instead," a boy
tells Rev. Lester Eisenberger.

Recreation at Jones Beach.

fear — precisely what the addicts were seeking in heroin.

One Rutgers University graduate student studied the relation of the conversion experience to rehabilitation at Teen Challenge. He concluded that at Teen Challenge it works — and better than motivation alone. As one addict told me, "Beautiful thoughts just aren't enough."

The permanence of this experience depends on personal faith, a faith which Teen Challenge tries to build through classes, chapel services, and counseling sessions. The daily classes are designed to teach the ABC's of Bible doctrine. In the chapel services the participants hear testimonies and sermons by various staff members and, on special occasions, speakers such as socialite Mrs. Eleanor Whitney and baseball pitchers Al Worthington and Jim Kaat. Counseling sessions with trained ministers help bring deep-seated emotional problems to the surface where they can be dealt with.

Rehabilitation is a process. It takes time. And, it takes money. Today, the operating expenses of the Brooklyn center alone amount to over $1,000 per day. Eighty percent of this budget is met by small gifts from numerous

Work and Bible classes teach discipline and principles of Christian living. A full schedule helps keep their minds off drugs and problems.

individuals, many of whom learned of Teen Challenge in the best seller by Rev. David Wilkerson, *The Cross and the Switchblade*, which sold over four million copies in twenty-eight languages.

David Wilkerson is no longer the director of the Brooklyn center as he was when he wrote *The Cross and the Switchblade* and several other books on Teen Challenge. "I never felt my work was administrative," said Dave. "I felt from the very beginning that my job was to be more or less a catalyst in launching programs and bringing together people who share this vision. I've helped launch Teen Challenge, the farm, the girls' home, the Bible school, the Cure Corps, and a children's program. As executive director, I turn these ministries over to others and I give spiritual counseling and guidance, then I chart another course somewhere."

Dave's brother, Don Wilkerson, is now directing the Brooklyn center. Beginning as a street worker with the Hellburners and the Roman Lords, gangs in Brooklyn, Don worked his way up through the ranks, holding numerous positions over the years.

During their two-month stay in Brooklyn, participants in the program will hear Don Wilkerson speak many times in chapel and at the well-attended Saturday evening rallies. Then they will go to "God's Mountain."

Rev. Don Wilkerson, director of the Brooklyn center, ponders whether to re-admit a dropout. Left: "You can tell when a boy is thinking about drugs, the street, or his family," commented one counselor. "You can see it in his eyes." Unless he is counseled immediately, he will likely leave.

"A paradise of inner tranquility seems to be faith's usual result; and it is easy, even without being religious one's self, to understand this. . . . And, indeed, how can it possibly fail to steady the nerves, to cool the fever, and appease the fret, if one be sensibly conscious that, no matter what one's difficulties for the moment may appear to be, one's life as a whole is in the keeping of a power whom one can absolutely trust?"

Dr. William James, Varieties of Religious Experience.

THE FARM

The Teen Challenge Training Center, affectionately called "God's Mountain" by those who have been there, is on a 210-acre farm in Rehrersburg, Pennsylvania. It is forty miles east of Harrisburg, within driving distance of New York City but far enough away to make a fellow think twice before leaving.

The training center was established in 1962 to provide an atmosphere of love and discipline in a rural setting. Without the distraction of the city, some sixty to eighty converted addicts now learn to live happy, successful Christian lives.

Rev. Frank Reynolds, the superintendent, and his twenty-seven staff members use Bible-centered classroom training, personal counseling, and strict discipline to build Christian character.

Each student spends at least three hours a day in the chapel or classroom, intensively studying the Bible and the elements of practical Christian living, such as standards of conduct, personal evangelism, the Christian home. Classes are conducted in both English and Spanish because seventy percent of those in the program are Spanish-speaking. In addition to Bible study, there are daily classes in English and Spanish grammar and literature. For those who need it, there is a course in remedial reading and grammar.

One of the most important lessons is not taught in the classroom; however, it is learned on the farm. Some critics think it is foolish to bring a product of the slums to the country. "There are no farms in Brooklyn," one lady said. "Why teach them to work on a farm?"

Rev. Frank Reynolds replied, "They have been involved with drugs since their teen years, so usually they haven't held steady jobs. The type of job they do isn't as important as learning to work. Before they came they hated work, but we try to show them there is pleasure and a sense of accomplishment in work."

To do this, the work program involves vocational training. The students have a choice of on-the-job training in auto mechanics, woodworking and carpentry, printing, dairy farming, cooking, office work, and cleaning and maintenance. Graduates are now using their classroom training and vocational skills at Teen Challenge centers around the country. In Los Angeles, for example, one man uses his auto repair training to maintain Teen Challenge vehicles; in Puerto Rico five former students help supervise the induction of addicts.

In addition to learning to work together, the men learn to live together. When several persons of different nationalities, steeped in prejudice and accustomed to violence, must share the same room one can expect trouble.

Surprisingly, though, few serious incidents have occurred at the farm. Rev. Robert Rainbow, the academic dean, attributes this to the work of the Holy Spirit in the students' lives.

When Pete came to the farm he was ready to handle his problems with his fists. In Puerto Rico he had been a street fighter; on the farm he became a woods fighter. At a chapel service six months after he arrived, he surrendered his life to God. There was a radical change in his life immediately apparent to all. Whereas before he had been aggressive and belligerent, now he would walk away from a disagreement rather than punch his antagonist.

What happened? Rev. Robert Rainbow, speaking of Pete and others like him, said, "After a period of teaching and training, the truth finally takes hold. The Scripture says it in this way: 'You shall know the truth and the the truth shall set you free.' (John 8:32 RSV). We feel that at this point intellectual faith becomes personal. Then progress begins."

Farmer-preacher Rev. Frank Reynolds speaks to "his boys" in chapel and jokes with several helping with the 5 A.M. chores.

By the time most go to the farm, they find the hymns are becoming personally meaningful. Their prayers consist of fewer agonizing pleas for help and more thanks for blessings given.

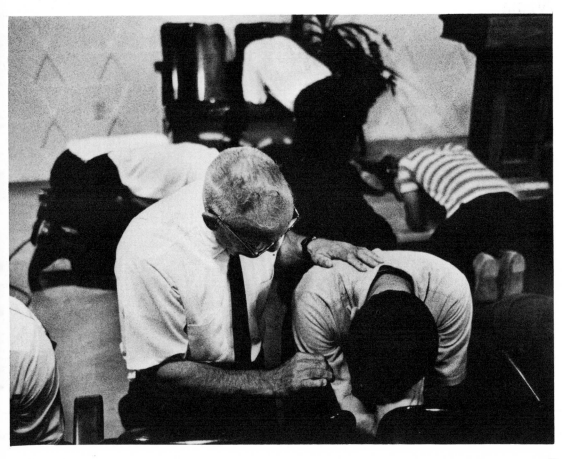

Rev. Robert Rainbow, academic dean.

Writing on a desktop.

The Spanish division is important as some speak no English.

Besides Bible, the basics of English grammar are taught.

*Books on Bible doctrine and
literature are popular
in the well-stocked library.*

During the first two months at the farm the program is new. It is a novelty. After they have made their first visit home, however, they must fight again the battle of the program versus the street. During that visit the wives of the married men often beg their husbands to remain at home. The married men then begin to think, "I should be home supporting my family." The fifth and sixth months are also critical. The men usually feel that by then they are strong enough as Christians to venture forth. If they leave, they will probably fall back into addiction; if they stay for a total of eight or nine months, they have more than a seventy percent chance of succeeding.

Those who leave before finishing the program almost always return to the spike. Several have tried to inject as much heroin as they used before, forgetting that the body had lost its tolerance to heroin. What was once normal became an O.D., and each died.

Others, more cautious at first, increased their dosage quickly to erase all thought of Teen Challenge and God. Simon, a dropout, told me, "When I went back to the street I was soon shooting up two and three times as much stuff to forget about what I learned here." He couldn't forget, so he returned.

Another boy said, "After I left, I walked around all the time with my face on the ground. If I looked up, I thought about God. I had to sleep on my stomach or side. I couldn't lie on my back because when I looked at the ceiling I'd think about God." After two miserable years of thinking about what he left at "God's Mountain" he also came back.

Each chooses the vocational field in which he wants to be trained, including dairy farming (left), woodworking and carpentry (above and right), mechanics, printing, cooking, office work and maintenance.

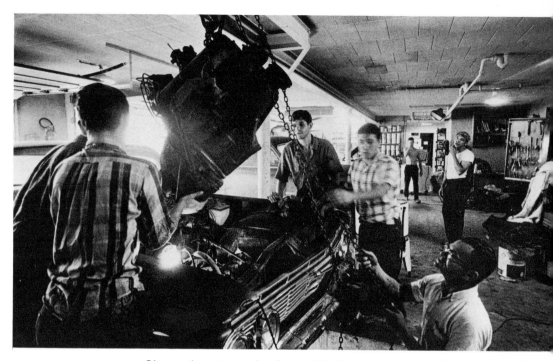

Classes in auto mechanics and body work are taught by professionals.

"They have to feel that you love them and that you are their friend regardless of what they've been or how they treat you at the present. If they know that you're honestly concerned about their problems they will listen."

Rev. Robert Rainbow

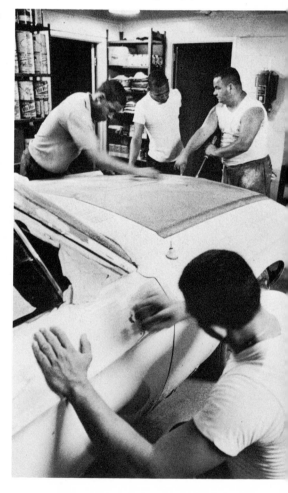

In addition to trying to persuade the impatient to stay, the staff spends considerable time counseling many on marriage and family problems. Some students have common-law wives who were not legally divorced from their former husbands. Before, there were no qualms about living together. Now, because the men are Christians, there is a conflict.

Because they are Christians they also have a tremendous concern for their families. Before, they stole from their families and caused much heartache, grief, and disappointment. Now, they want to make restitution. And they want their families to know Christ. Many students return to the farm saying that several relatives — and occasionally, entire families — have been converted because of their testimonies.

In one instance a student had to say very

Students learn basic printing on jobs done for the farm and businesses.

Thirty-seven converts are baptized in the farm pond after each testifies.

The converts, withdrawn and insecure at first, show more interest in each other and visitors as they progress in their Christian lives.

little. Louis had been an addict for seven years. His sister, a psychologist in the New York school system, spent thousands of dollars trying to rehabilitate him. At times she even bought heroin for him herself so he wouldn't be arrested. Twice she administered it to him in smaller and smaller doses, hoping to wean him from his habit.

Finally, hearing of Teen Challenge, she brought him into the Brooklyn center on a Monday. On Thursday he was taken to the farm. (This was when the program first began. Now, he would stay at the Brooklyn center several months.) His sister was at the center to say good-by.

Five days later she came to the farm to visit him. There had been such a dramatic physical change in Louis that although she was well-educated and normally unemotional, she let out a scream and began to weep when she saw him. Rev. Frank Reynolds said, "She hugged him and kissed him and patted him and pushed him away and looked at him again and cried. It was one of the most thrilling things in my life to be there to ob-

serve it. That night she also gave her heart to the Lord. And Louis received the baptism of the Holy Spirit."

Many of the men at the farm find the Pentecostal charismatic experience a turning point. "The baptism" seems to make temptations less menacing and God more real.

" 'What's in it for me?' is what a drug addict thinks. His world revolves around himself. The Christian's life is different. His world revolves around others."

Rev. Frank Reynolds

Concerning the Holy Spirit, David Wilkerson has said, "Certainly we cannot claim a magical cure for dope addiction. The devil which hides in that needle is so deadly strong that any such claim would be folly. All we can say, perhaps, is that we have found a power which captures a boy more strongly than narcotics. But that power is the Holy Spirit Himself, which, unlike narcotics, does a strange thing for our boys: He captures only to liberate."

After the converts have completed the course on Fundamentals of the Faith, they

Now in re-entry, Santiago M. (pictured withdrawing on p. 30) counsels a newcomer recovering from a bullet wound inflicted by another addict.

are candidates for water baptism. These services are held occasionally at the farm's pond.

Those who are progressing spiritually give their testimonies at many churches on weekends. During the week they speak in high schools and colleges, where religion is often taboo. "These people get shook," one staff worker said. "We come in and show them what God has done in a drug addict's life and they can't explain it. The can't put it in a test tube."

When a staff worker evaluates a convert for spiritual progress, he looks not only for understanding of the Bible, but also for a genuine concern for others. The drug addict's world revolves around himself; a Christian's world revolves around others. A committed Christian must be willing to assume responsibility and to face up to reality.

Upon completion of the program, a convert will probably stay clean. In 1966 Rev. Frank Reynolds went through his file of those who had come into the program since 1963. He was certain that of the 131 who had completed the program, 71.4 percent were not using drugs in any form. His study is now being updated by a staff member trained in statistics. It looks as if the current percentage of those "living victoriously" will be several points higher.

About half of those who complete the program go on to Bible school. Some want to train for the ministry, while others want to further their education. Some just want the additional discipline a Bible school atmosphere provides. They usually find that the eight or nine months spent at the training center is equivalent to about two semesters at Bible school.

At one time it was very difficult for some converts to enter Bible college because they could not meet entrance requirements. As a result, the Teen Challenge Institute of Missions was established.

There are now many opportunities for the converts to further their education, but what happens to those who don't want to go on to school? It would be disheartening for a boy to be thrown out onto the street with no place to go but his old neighborhood. There, all of his friends still shoot heroin. If he can't find a job because of his past, he might stop resisting his friends and resort to the same old escape route.

To meet this problem the Brooklyn center established the re-entry program. This program permits converts to remain in a Christian family-type environment while they re-establish themselves. About twenty live in the re-entry home for a nominal rent. They are helped to find jobs and, from the first pay check on, are required to save systematically. Willie proudly made his first deposit — five dollars — with the help of a staff worker. Before, while he was pushing heroin, he had always kept his money — up to $17,000 — stashed in a shoe box.

The re-entry converts are required to attend several Teen Challenge services and a church of their choice. Some of them go to church with more than spiritual interests in mind. As Santiago said, "When I was a junkie, all I cared about was dope. I didn't have time for girls. But now. . . ."

Socially, physically and spiritually revived, these are the Awakened Dead.

The men will eventually leave re-entry either
alone, or like Angelo Diaz, with a Christian
wife. Angelo says, "My family cried when they
heard I was getting married because they didn't
think I would ever change." This is under-
standable. Until 1967, Angelo's thirteen-year
nightmare included eight OD's, one attempt at
suicide, many arrests for burglary,
possession of heroin, armed robbery and attempted
murder. Once he managed to stay clean from
heroin by drinking heavily to relax, but the
experiment ended with Angelo losing a barroom
brawl with five men and a crowbar. He then
lived on rooftops and in basements — cold, hungry,
and lonely — until a friend told him about Christ
and Christians who cared. Later, at the farm,
he met Nellie, a visitor. She says, "We started
talking about God. We gave each other our
testimonies and today here we are." She is
teaching him to read and write (a teacher once
told him he would need a specialist to teach him). Angelo
says, "Before, I had complexes. I was scared
to talk to anyone. Now, even when I get
behind a pulpit I'm relaxed. I know that
God wants to use me as a minister."

HOVING HOME

The female addict (who makes up about twenty percent of the total) may support her habit by shoplifting and forging checks. Almost inevitably, however, the girls — even the proud, the religious, the respectable — turn to prostitution. As one girl, a college graduate, said, "Heroin is something else. It takes you to the point where you'd kill your own mother for a fix."

In New York City the prostitutes are legion. On just one of the many blocks in Manhattan they frequent, a policeman said that over fifty had been arrested the night before. Probably over half of these were addicts.

Numbers, however, do not tell the story of an addicted girl's anguish. One midnight in Harlem I saw a bedraggled Spanish girl lean against a lamppost as she desperately watched the cars driving by. Her arms clutched her stomach as she shook with withdrawal chills. Bitterly, pitifully, she sobbed at the pain, knowing that as long as tears streamed down her cheeks no one would buy her, but without that money her pain and tears would last many hours.

On the same block Johnny Melendez and I met Midge. We had been talking to several addicts when we saw her. Sharply dressed, she looked like a college sophomore, which she would have been if she hadn't quit to support her habit. Eight months before, her boy friend had given her her first shot.

Four months after we met her, we saw her again. She had aged ten years. Her dress was a rag; her hair was a mop. She had lost thirty pounds and her front teeth to a sadistic customer. She had been in jail twice and in the hospital twice, once after someone had tried to kill her. A mentally unbalanced "trick" (customer) had shot her three times. Luckily none of the wounds was serious.

At twenty-one she is one of the walking dead, or perhaps one of the buried dead. If so, few would mourn: she is a junkie and a prostitute.

"Maybe we're alive, but man, we ain't livin'. We're junkies ... zombies. Everybody hates us. But these people from Teen Challenge, they don't just see us as dirty junkies and prostitutes. To them we're people, human beings. And that's really something."

Eighteen-year-old prostitute.

Rosa was a businesswoman, not by choice but by necessity. She sold everything she could steal to pawnshops. To any willing customer she sold her body and envelopes of white oblivion.

This afternoon she was replenishing her supply of the latter. A connection was bringing her four "bundles" of heroin — one hundred "nickle" bags. She sat on a car hood waiting in front of one of the many tenements that line Fox Street in the "Little Korea" section of the Bronx. Impatiently Rosa glanced at the many people on the fire escapes, tenement steps, and sidewalks. Suddenly she noticed a friend, a former cell mate, who was carrying a big black book.

"Hi, Carmen. What are you doing now, stealing Bibles?"

Carmen began to cry. Wiping her eyes, she told Rosa she was clean, that God had helped

An 18-year-old prostitute, a heroin user, waits for a customer on a Brooklyn street corner. Many young girls are forced into prostitution by addiction.

"Maybe a doctor could find a vein, but I can't," says a twenty-six-year-old girl as she injects three bags of heroin into skin tissue. Her surface veins have collapsed, and she has many abscesses from dirty needles and impure drugs.

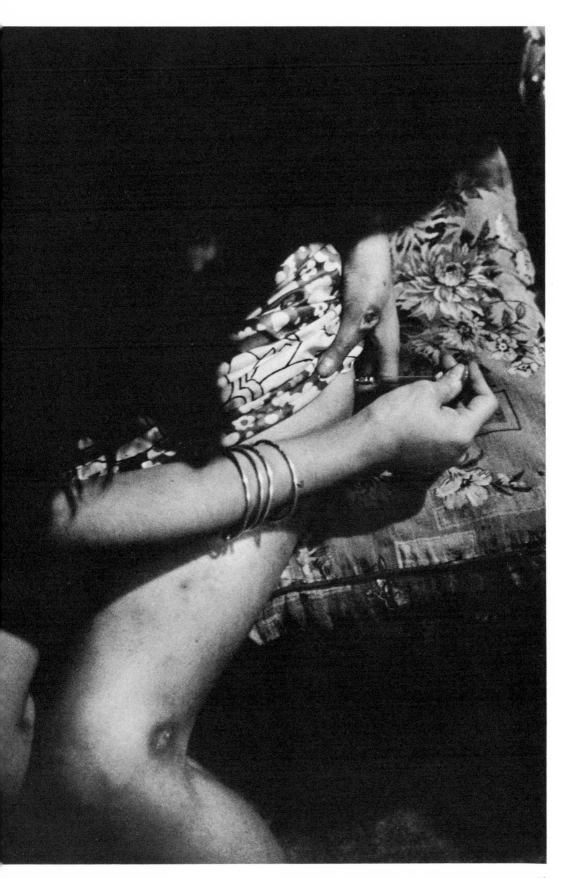

The Walter Hoving Home for Girls, Garrison, N.Y.

her and that He would do the same for Rosa.

Rosa didn't believe it. She knew she was hopeless. Even a psychiatrist had told her that she would always be addicted; but Rosa saw something was different about Carmen, and that she also looked healthier. Rosa, a scrawny ninety-five pounds, thought "Nothing can cure me, but at least I can put on some weight." So she followed Carmen to Teen Challenge.

Rosa still spends much of her time on the streets, but now like Carmen she carries a big black book and tells her old friends that God will help them as well.

Except for minor details, Rosa's story is not much different from the stories of other girls who have completed the rehabilitation program at the Walter Hoving Home for Girls. Rosa came to Teen Challenge expecting nothing but a bed and three meals. However, she had a personal experience with Christ, and after she finished the program she went to Bible school. Now she is happily married.

The Walter Hoving Home for Girls (named in honor of a long-time Teen Challenge friend, the chairman of the board of Tiffany's) is located on a beautiful estate in Garrison, New York. Here some seventeen troubled girls are housed in a family-type atmosphere. The staff of nine is supervised by Rev. John Benton, associate director of Teen Challenge.

The girls' program is similar to the boys'. Prime importance is placed on spiritual therapy through conversion to Christ, and through prayer, Bible study, chapel worship, and per-

sonal counseling.

As at the Brooklyn center, most of those admitted originally were drug addicts and abusers. In December, 1967, there were fifteen girls in the program, including ten addicts and abusers, two delinquents, one unwed mother, and two who had emotional problems. Occasionally, runaways and hippies are admitted.

Some girls leave the first few days because they don't want to kick cold turkey or give up cigarettes. A few return. Because she wasn't allowed to smoke, Louise vowed she'd never come back. Two days later she phoned Rev. John Benton asking to be readmitted. When she went home her five-year-old daughter told her, "Mommie, we don't want you anymore." The heartbroken mother decided she had to conquer her habit — even if it meant giving up cigarettes.

Those who stay in the program begin a gradual rehabilitation process. As with the men, they are encouraged to accept Christ, preferably not in a sudden burst of emotion. According to Miss Terri Avila, the assistant director, those who have a sudden emotional response and seem to progress by leaps and bounds often fizzle. Emotion for emotion's sake is not encouraged.

Sometimes a girl's progress is so gradual that it goes unnoticed. Phyllis, who was known for her violent temper, said, "I blew my top when a girl aggravated me yesterday. Ordinarily I wouldn't have just gotten mad. I would have hit her with a chair — really. But even though my feelings were hurt and my pride was hurt I went and prayed. Then someone put her hands in my face and

During rehabilitation the girls require much more individual attention and counseling than the boys.

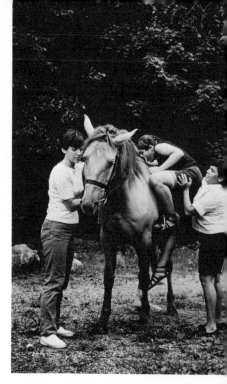

*Success Motivation supplements Bible classes
in aiding personality and character development.*

"This booklet has meant a great deal to me."

A campfire devotional service.

told me, 'Smell this.' And I didn't hit her neither. Now, I can actually pray for people when they hurt me. Before, I really hated them and wanted to get even.'' Phyllis' violent temper stemmed from years of living on the street, where only the tough survive.

Another problem that results from street life is guilt. When the men become Christians and make restitution for their crimes they are usually not haunted by the past. This is not so with the women. Whether a girl is a college graduate or a Sunday school teacher, heroin almost certainly forces her into prostitution. Involvement in prostitution often leads to an intense hatred of men, and then lesbianism. The guilt and shame are not easily erased. Converted girls hesitate to refer to their past because, as I overheard one tell another, ''People don't even think we're human.''

*Maria Santiago testifies to visitors. Two years
before she had cursed Reverend Benton and had tried
to pick his pocket. "I thought he was nuts telling
me that Jesus Christ could solve my problems,"
she says. Addicted two years at seventeen, even $60 of
heroin daily could not keep her high, so she tried
pills too. The pills caused disastrous memory
lapses. She would often lure a man into a hallway
to mug him, and the next day, not remembering,
follow him again to be brutally beaten. The
pills made her violent. After being slashed by an
addict, she left her assailant with stab wounds
which took 149 stitches to close. Maria was
brought to Teen Challenge by a minister when she
became sick. She stayed a month to physically
kick three habits, heroin, pills, and cigarettes,
but then she went back to the street. Heroin
could not supply the inner peace she had
just found so she returned. Now in Bible school,
she is a radiant Christian. Reverend Benton says,
"If I'm ever tempted to doubt that there is a
God, one word would change my mind — Maria."*

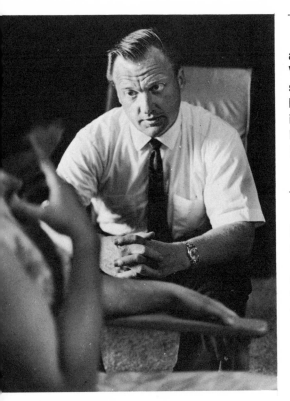

Rev. John Benton counsels a girl.

"My mother went to my water baptism and cried. I'd never seen her cry before. When I was coming out of the water, she said that it was the first time in her life that she could see sincerity in me. She said she could tell by the look on my face that I had found what I was seeking for all these years."

Converted addict and prostitute.

"Actually, once the girls are separated from their habits, they're basically the same as other girls," said Rev. John Benton.

Through hours of prayer, Bible classes, and counseling, their self-respect slowly returns, and their individual hang-ups are mastered. Another aid, a recent addition to the curriculum, is Success Motivation. This class is designed to motivate the women to their fullest potential, develop their personalities, and supplement the Bible class in dealing with their fears and personal problems. The staff feels that this course is also motivating some girls to finish the program. Since the course was begun, the drop-out rate has fallen significantly.

Although the girls' problems seem to hang heavier than the boys' problems, they usually perk up when asked, "What has God done for you?" One woman, an addict for ten years, began to sparkle. "You know, it's just fabulous that we can be with God. As big as He is — He fills the whole universe — He has time to come and be with us. It's a miracle — that's all it is — it's a miracle.

"I'm so happy. To think that I used to be smoking and drinking and shooting dope and running around Skid Row and stealing from people and looking like a bum and not caring about life and unhappy. Now I've never been so happy in my life. Praise God. He's done wonders for me.

"Some people might think that it's fanatical to feel this way, but I think I'd rather be a fanatic than a dope addict or prostitute or what have you."

Hundreds of others have been through the Teen Challenge program. They agree.

BIBLE SCHOOL

"Father, our meat and milk are nearly gone. Please send some. Thank you," a girl prays near a classmate's Bible and bookmark. Their faith is sometimes put to a practical test.

A T.C.I.M. student studies along the bank of the Hudson River, near the school.

An ex-addict wanted to go to Bible school. His qualifications were an eighth-grade trade-school education, an employment record as a burglar and narcotics dealer with many arrests and convictions, and only a few character references (the one prosperous businessman he knew was a numbers racketeer). Until the year before, his hobbies had been shooting dope, shooting crap and shooting cops. Very likely he would need extensive counseling.

Would any school accept him? Until April, 1966, probably not. Then the Teen Challenge Institute of Missions opened as the finishing touch of the rehabilitation program.

In this school the Bible is the basic text and the staff continues the work of remolding character, renewing minds, and restoring social responsibility. This is not just another Bible school. Its purpose is to equip students to be competent Teen Challenge workers and useful Christians.

David Wilkerson has said, "We are not only interested in saving the lives of delinquents, addicts, and prostitutes, but we are also determined to train them to go back into the streets with us. We must reach thousands more."

The school is located near the Hudson River on a former Astor estate in Rhinebeck, New York. To David Wilkerson and Nicky Cruz the stone mansion and surrounding one hundred acres seemed to be God's answer for a girls' home some years ago. It was acquired in the same manner as most Teen Challenge buildings: it seemed to fill a desperate need, so the papers were signed even though there was no money to pay for it.

*Teen Challenge Institute
of Missions; Rhinebeck, N.Y.*

*A teacher helps a student
with his homework*

English class.

Rev. John Kenzy, superintendent.

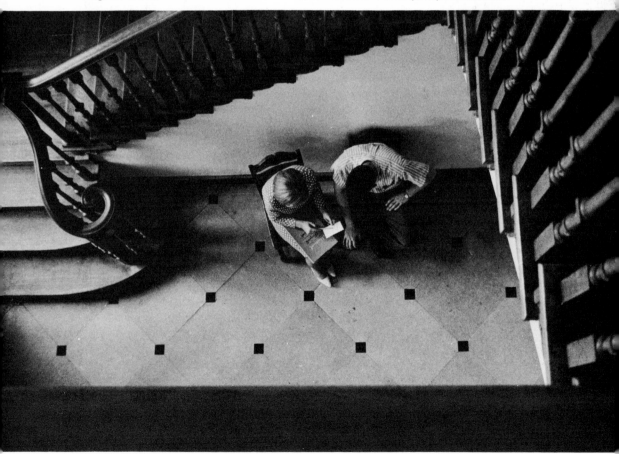

David Wilkerson knew God wanted them to have it, and eventually the bill was paid.

After a period of time Dave realized that the estate was too secluded for a girls' home, but that it would meet another urgent need — a Bible school.

When the first trimester began the school had a student body of nine. The faculty of two couples was Rev. Edmund Cooksey, the superintendent, and Rev. John Kenzy, the dean, and their wives. In January, 1969, Rev. John Kenzy became the superintendent

"They're not just teachers to us. They're more like parents — a lot better to us than our own, really."

Student at T.C.I.M.

---

of the school, which had mushroomed to an enrollment of forty-two. Both students and staff were crammed into every possible space, including the attic, walk-in closets, and the garage. Living conditions will be less crowded and the enrollment will increase to 100 as soon as a dormitory and staff quarters are constructed.

The students are as varied as the people who come to Teen Challenge for help. In addition to some thirty ex-addicts, pillheads and alcoholics, eight of the students have been hippies, a number were homosexuals and lesbians, several were delinquents and some have had severe emotional problems. Their educational backgrounds vary also. Some completed only grade school; others attended or graduated from high school. One girl was a college graduate who became so

psychologically dependent on marijuana that she "almost went nuts" when her supply of pot ran out while visiting relatives overseas.

In the six-trimester two-year course, the students study typical Bible school subjects, such as numerous courses on Bible content and doctrine, evangelism, missions, preaching, English, and United States and world history. These courses are taught with the student's background and future service in mind. Some plan to go on for further academic training. Some will leave for secular jobs. Most will become workers at Teen

A Bible school is a combination of academic and spiritual. While he was an addict, this boy probably never noticed a sunset.

An ex-hippie from California strums and studies in her room. Like several others, she enrolled because of the school's spiritual atmosphere and training, rather than for rehabilitation.

Challenge centers across the country after graduation.

New subjects for prospective Teen Challenge workers recently added to the curriculum include Hygiene (basic first aid, medical terms, and procedures a person working with addicts needs to know), Clerical Training (typing, shorthand, bookkeeping), Marriage and Family Relations, Journalism, Court Procedures (methods for working on court cases), and Christian Conduct (manners, customs).

In addition to the lenient entrance requirements and some unique courses, the Institute is unusual in another respect. Students pay only thirty-two dollars for room, board and tuition each trimester. This is possible because each student is required to work three hours a day. The girls cook, sew, do housekeeping, and work in the recently-established publications department. The boys maintain the buildings and grounds, and will soon be working in a new farming program. Those who cannot afford fees can work overtime.

The students get practical experience on weekends by sharing their testimonies and counseling on the streets, in jails, and at the hospitals of nearby communities. They also help conduct services in a home mission church.

The staff is naturally anxious for each student to progress academically, but they also expect that the classes, counseling, discipline, and spiritual atmosphere will have a personal effect on each student. This effect is, as one teacher said, "to get their religion out of their emotions and into their attitudes and actions." When this happens, each student will become not only a stable, successful Christian, but an asset to society as well.

Required work helps keep tuition and fees very low.

Greenwich Village,
haven for frolicking hippies, teeny-boppers,
alcoholics and homosexuals, gaping
tourists and beleaguered residents.

THE LOST COIN

Paralyzed by fear, a pretty thirteen-year-old runaway locked herself into the East Village crash pad in which she was staying. She was paranoid, and afraid she would be identified and returned home by the police or arrested by a "nark," (a narcotics agent). After a week her fear passed and she went outside again.

The police did locate Laurie a few weeks later; by that time she had contracted a venereal disease, had been beaten up by a group of hippie-hating Puerto Ricans, and had discovered that her best friend was a nark. He rented the crash pad in which she had locked herself. Laurie admitted later that the Village is a "bummer" (something bad), but she preferred it and the friends she couldn't trust, to the hassles at home.

She was but one of the 10,000 runaways who invaded Greenwich Village in 1967 searching for fun and freedom and finding little of either. A few wandered into The Lost Coin, the Teen Challenge coffeehouse-style dialogue center, and left — different persons.

Ronnie came in one night. After being challenged by a tract and a counselor, he agreed that Christ could solve his problems. He returned home to his parents.

One pretty eighteen-year-old was about to run away when she talked to Mrs. Ann Wilkerson, mother of David Wilkerson. According to the girl, her parents were bugging her. She said, "We have nothing to talk about — just nothing." So she was going to run away. Mrs. Wilkerson encouraged her to begin with a right relationship with God. After they prayed together the girl left with a New Testament. She returned a few weeks later to thank Mrs. Wilkerson for her prayer and counseling. She too had found that a right relationship with God helped her family relations.

Not all who come into The Lost Coin want to change. Two young runaways from New Hampshire agreed with one worker that the Bible has some beautiful things to say about such an experience. Then one commented, "It sounds groovy, but if I accepted Christ, I know God would want me to go home. And I'm not ready to do that yet."

In 1963 Mrs. Wilkerson joined with Faye Mianulli, a Village resident, to distribute Christian literature in Washington Square. Together they opened the Catacomb Chapel in what had been the Den of 40 Thieves, a

Roger Dean, who ministers at the Lost Coin, talks to a homosexual. For years a homo himself, Roger was converted at Teen Challenge in San Francisco. He has since married and has helped others break with "gay" life. How? "Romans 6 and II Corinthians 5:17," he says.

The Village attracts homosexuals, stag and drag.

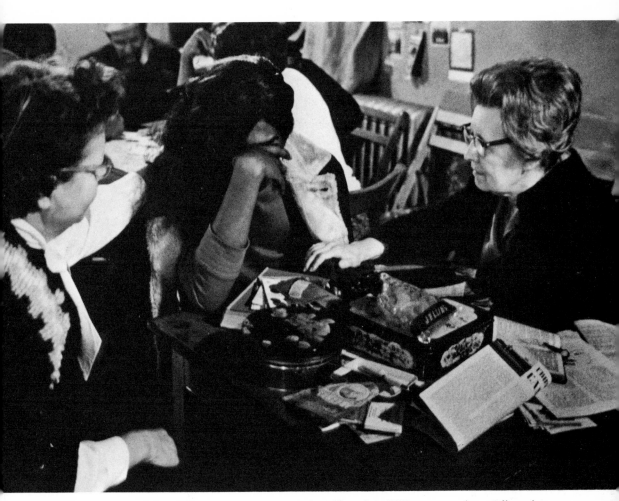

"I feel like I'm an animal," sobs a male homosexual to Mrs. Ann Wilkerson and a staff worker.

MacDougal Street coffeehouse. Eventually they were evicted on the charge: "You draw all the undesirables."

Faye and "Mom," as Mrs. Wilkerson is often affectionately called, then leased the Sullivan Street location and named their bookroom dialogue center The Lost Coin.

"We still have just as many undesirables," said Faye, "but we don't see them that way." These so-called undesirables include alcoholics from a nearby flophouse, weekend hippies, runaways and homosexuals. Frequently, weekend tourists also stop in. A few of those who come in do so to harass the workers and some want to discuss doctrine, but most wander in out of curiosity. All are challenged to have a personal encounter with Christ.

Their reactions vary. Some are indifferent; some are eager; some are antagonistic and even obscene.

Pessimists might label The Lost Coin "The Lost Cause," because many of the converts are not heard of again. Mrs. Wilkerson said, "This is a transient ministry. These young people come and go and after one conversation we may never see them again."

The workers are not discouraged, however, because reports of changed lives do filter back. One teen-age girl, who would today be called a teeny-bopper, occasionally came in for counseling. She later returned to say that she had come to know the Lord and was attending a Bible college. For this girl The Lost Coin was certainly not a Lost Cause.

CHILDREN

Loneliness. Boredom. These are problems for any youngster or teenager, but in the ghetto they are magnified by hunger, danger, disease, prejudice, and mistreatment.

Because of loneliness and boredom many teens once joined fighting gangs. More recently, alarming numbers of slum youths have turned to chemical friends.

"Sometimes I'd get so miserable that I'd go out and sit on the curb and cry," said Demi, a fourteen-year-old boy. He lived in a small Brooklyn apartment with his parents, his source of misery. "I thought they didn't want me, so I went out and took pills and things." The pills were goofballs — barbiturates. The "things" were liquor, marijuana, glue and heroin. According to Demi, many of his friends, including his thirteen-year-old girl friend, took heroin because they felt unloved and lonely.

Teddy, a fourteen-year-old from the Bronx, wasn't lonely or unloved. "I just wanted to get high, you know, just for kicks," he said. To get his high, he would occasionally snort cocaine or skin-pop heroin. Mostly he sniffed glue. He wasn't ignorant of the dangers involved, because one day while sniffing with Georgie, a sixteen-year-old friend, Georgie screamed that flying saucers were after him and jumped off the roof, six stories high. Teddy said, "He went through a garage roof and all you could see was half of his head. He busted a lot of bones but he lived. And he still sniffs glue."

Teddy also got some kicks stealing cars ("Like it's my profession. I've stolen maybe 20 or 25") and fighting. His problem, like many other delinquents, was boredom. He said, "The kids in the city don't have hardly nothing to do. The [recreation] centers aren't open each day, you know, so they're looking for something to do and they end up stealing and getting high and stuff like that."

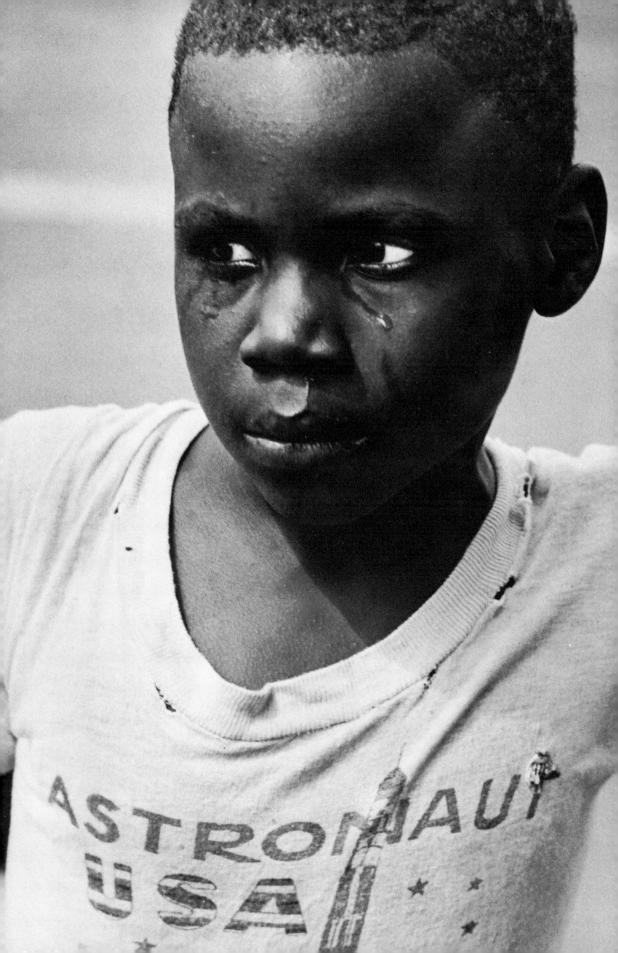

A Brooklyn child searches each can for food or toys. Below: Spanish Harlem.

Right: A staff worker and two friends splash at a Staten Island picnic for kids who attended T.C. Bible classes. Many of the 40 children had never before seen a beach and had to be carried into the water. For some, this was their first auto ride.

YOUTH HOMES

David Wilkerson wept when two baby girls were brought into the center by a street evangelism team. Their bodies were covered with marks of neglect. Both had been treated for scald burns and shock after one had overturned a steaming kettle of water into their crib. Their mother, an addict, had passed out on her bed while trying to kick cold turkey. Even when she was conscious she didn't pay much attention to them. Their pitifully thin bodies were covered with lice and sores. The younger girl's diapers hadn't been changed in days, and the older girl wore only an undershirt, many sizes too small.

It wasn't the first time Reverend Wilkerson and his staff had seen horribly mistreated children of addicts, but this time he decided to do something about it. His plan was to set up group homes in a campus-type setting with plenty of space for the kids to play. Each home would be a separate family with eight or ten children, house parents, and a staff worker or two.

Phase one of Dave's dream went into effect March 1, 1967. The Teen Challenge Little People's Home was opened in Westbury, Long Island, with Charles and Barbara Miller as the house parents.

For eighteen months the Little People's Home operated as an experimental, temporary shelter providing Christian love, discipline, and guidance to the youngsters in its care.

As was anticipated, problems arose. One thirteen-year-old girl had homicidal tendencies. She loved the violence she had known at home on Manhattan's Lower East Side. She threatened to kill everyone at the home

Little Julio, who lived at the Little People's Home, was born addicted. He had to undergo withdrawal at birth because his mother was an addict.

and, before she was asked to leave, she had stolen a kitchen knife, perhaps in order to carry out her threats. A young teen-age boy bought marijuana from an eleven-year-old girl, a dealer at his school, and smuggled it into the home. Much more common were disciplinary problems, such as smoking by the teen-agers, lying and fighting.

Most of the children who came into the home sensed God's presence during devotions, and some asked God to come into their lives. But it takes time to mold a young life, especially after years of abuse and neglect. And time was one of the Millers' greatest problems.

It was discouraging to see a bewildered, mixed-up child begin to respond to love and then leave. One seven-year-old boy was sent to the home by his mother, a prostitute, who said, "He's as nervous as a wild animal." After several months, he no longer was edgy and he no longer beat up his classmates. There was such a change in him that when he went home for a visit his mother wouldn't let him leave. "He's not sad anymore," she said. Today he is at home and as miserable as ever.

The Westbury home was only a temporary shelter because it could not be certified by the state without a professional staff. Likewise, the Teen Challenge foster child placement program was only temporary, but it was temporary by necessity. Many of the children that were placed in New York City area homes were the children of men and women enrolled in the Teen Challenge program. When their parents finished the program, the children left to rejoin their parents.

Plans are now being made for a more permanent and thorough residence ministry for troubled youth. This ministry, now called David Wilkerson Youth Homes, is directed by Paul Duncan, a professional social worker who has served with the Mississippi Department of Public Welfare and as director of social services at the Church of God Children's Home in Tennessee.

The immediate plans are to obtain in Suffolk and Nassau counties, Long Island, three residential group homes similar to the Little People's Home. Each will house a maximum of seven youths, ten-to-seventeen-year-old delinquents and pre-delinquents. Ultimately the homes will serve as intake (and re-entry) centers for young people going to Teen Town, an ultramodern residential treatment center to be constructed on a 150-acre site at Orlando, Florida.

"We call it 'a place to grow' spiritually, physically, and mentally," said David Wilkerson. One hundred (and eventually three hundred) boys and girls will be stimulated to learn at Teen Town's own school by the latest educational techniques, especially audiovisual aids.

Like the boys' and girls' drug rehabilitation programs, Teen Town will seek to surround its kids with Christian love, security and discipline. But there is a difference. Teen Town will attempt to reach them before they're hooked, before they join the walking dead.

A family hymn-sing.

The Little People's Home, Westbury, L.I.

David Wilkerson and Paul Duncan discuss plans for Teen Town, the latest T.C. project.

TENEMENT HOUSE EVANGELISM

Bible studies are conducted in the homes of nearby children, men in the rehabilitation program and others, such as one teen-age girl who wrote, "I would appreciate information on getting ready to meet God." She, her mother, two sisters, a brother and several friends have become Christians through their Bible class.

FOSTER CHILD PROGRAM

A one-year-old girl meets her temporary foster parents. Some months later, her father married and was able to reclaim her. The foster child program was initiated to provide temporary Christian homes for children of parents enrolled in the rehabilitation program. Many of these children had spent all of their young lives being shuffled among unconcerned relatives.

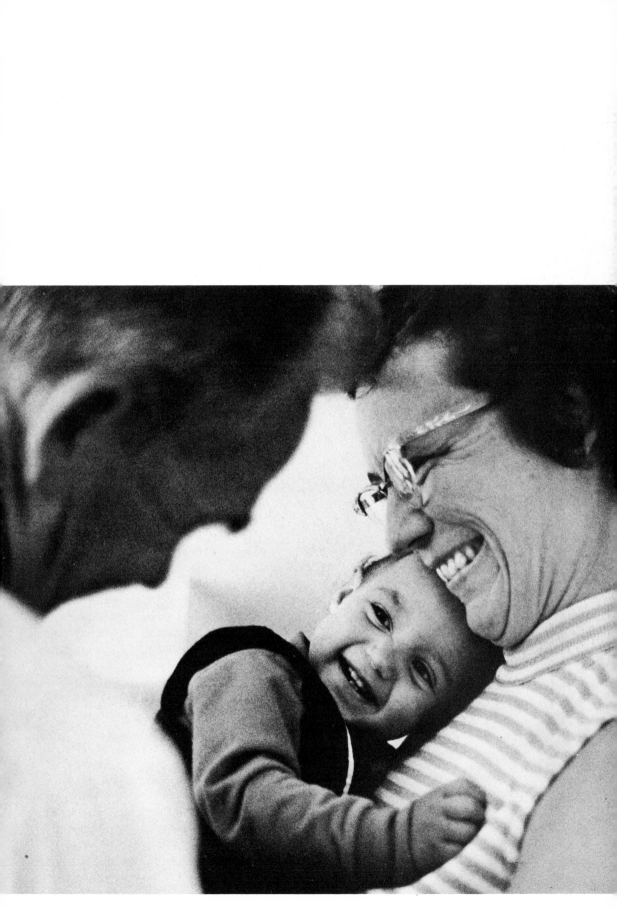

THE WELL

*In December, 1967 Rev. David Brett, then evangelism
director of Teen Challenge, rented a store front
in a derelict building in Brooklyn. After days of
work, The Well opened its doors to the neighborhood youth. The nightly Bible studies, games and
snacks were popular immediately. One group of
boys called The Rats promised, "If anybody messes
with this place we'll kill him."*

*They hadn't counted on the opposition — racketeers
running a gambling operation in the basement below.
When five men with shotguns robbed them of an
evening's take, the gamblers suspected the newcomers
above. Their suspicions seemed confirmed when the
treasury department began investigating. The men
ransacked The Well, then set fire to the building.
Understandably discouraged, Dave Brett removed the
lock (pictured at the left), all that was left. But
within days, four community centers opened their
doors to Teen Challenge workers, an unprecedented
move. David (pictured above) said, "As a result of
the fire, our ministry increased tenfold."*

CURE CORPS

A CURE Corps New Start class sings a favorite gospel chorus.

"We are here to show the city that we care because God cares, and to make His name known through faith coupled with hard work."

On July 1, 1968 the Collegiate Urban Renewal Effort began working in the notorious Fox Street section of the Bronx. Founder David Wilkerson had been troubled that the evangelical church seemed to avoid the dingy high-rise canyons of the ghetto, so he founded a Peace Corps-style agency for Christians who want to become involved.

Fox Street teens sneered at the team of fifteen college students and graduates, "You won't last longer than the others — maybe a few months." However, ten months later, Fox Street CURE and two other units (in the Brownsville and Bedford-Stuyvesant areas of Brooklyn) are conducting New Start classes for ninety pre-school kids, seven clubs (Red, Blue and Pink Berets) for grammar and high-school youth, three teen-age Bible study clubs, two adult Bible studies and camping excursions for the Beret clubs.

In the next few months CURE will attempt to increase its saturation to establish groups of believers. Also, workers will begin a community aid service, counseling on legal, employment, health, housing and other resources available.

Thus far, lonely children have been befriended, teens have found friends who will listen and help with homework, and a few are able to sing a new song, like a tiny New Start pupil who was hanging out of a tenement window and singing at the top of her lungs, "I'm so happy for Jesus is a friend of mine."

"Miss Phyllis, I did it!"
proclaims a proud New Start pupil
after being shown how to color.

CAMPING

In the summer of 1967 Teen Challenge initiated a summer camping program for underprivileged girls. Each week during the summer as many as thirty-five teen-age girls living in New York City's ghetto areas attended a free week of camp. Located on the grounds of the Walter Hoving Home, this camp was designed to meet both the spiritual and physical needs of girls before they became enmeshed in drug addiction.

According to Theo Edwards, the camp's director, the main objectives were "to lead each person to Jesus Christ and to teach her how to work and get along with others — in short, practical Christianity." Each day Theo taught a class on the Bible. Using the Bible as a text she and the campers investigated such topics as what sin is, who Jesus Christ is, and what it means to have a changed life.

To test the counselors, the girls often played practical jokes. One group put Ajax in the counselors' hair while they were sleeping. Once the counselors had proved themselves, however, the girls shared their problems and sought advice.

Participating in one session for young campers were two girls dating boys back home who were mainlining heroin, the sister of an addicted prostitute who was herself experimenting with drugs, a girl who had emotional problems caused by an extremely unhappy home life, and several girls who smoked marijuana regularly.

The activities at the camp helped the girls to get their minds off their troubles. There they could choose what they liked to do. Theo found that most of the girls preferred to swim, go horseback riding or hiking rather than paint pictures or weave baskets. In one group, four of the seven campers had never ridden a bicycle, so they spent much of their free time trying to stay on top of one. They went home with skinned elbows and knees but thrilled that they had learned to ride a bicycle.

After the girls left, Theo wrote each a letter and enclosed a booklet on living a successful Christian life.

Some of the girls have returned in the winter for weekend camping, a real thrill for slum girls. Because it's impossible to build a snowman on a fire escape or go tobogganing in a busy city street, the winter campers spend a great deal of time outside in the snow, sledding, having snowball fights, building snow castles and hiking.

During the weekend camping sessions Theo was able to encourage and counsel each girl further. She was anxious to see how each girl was progressing in her Christian life.

There are indications that some of the girls will never be quite the same as they were before. Rev. John Benton was fixing a lawn mower on the side of a hill when he overheard two girls talking. Mary, a fourteen-year-old who had been smoking pot regularly and hanging out with a bad crowd,

A dip in a pool fed by a mountain stream is a treat for girls who have known only tenements and busy city streets.

remarked to another camper, "Man, when I get back to the city, I'm not gonna do the things I used to."

The minister said, "I wondered how well she would really turn out."

Mary attended the Teen Challenge Saturday night rally regularly and one night brought a rough-looking friend. At the close of the service Rev. John Benton, who was praying with several campers at the altar, turned around and saw Mary, fervently praying with her friend.

"I think this is a real endorsement of what God can do," Rev. John Benton now says. "Mary has not moved. She lives in the same neighborhood, but her life is different."

Counselor Theo Edwards receives a surprise. The girls enjoy practical jokes, usually more than Theo.

*Classes in Bible and
practical Christianity
are important
parts of the curriculum.*

YOUTH CRUSADES

During half time at a basketball game Linda Campbell's best girl friend took a pistol from her pocketbook and shot herself in the stomach. The last words she muttered as she died in Linda's arms were, "Nobody cares." She was fifteen.

Several months later Linda, still badly shaken, sobbed her story to David Wilkerson.

Since 1964 Dave has counseled thousands of middle class teens with problems, some as tragic as Linda's. In that year he began holding meetings, "crusades" he calls them, for goodniks — restless, bored, middle class youth. He immediately found that kids in the ghetto don't have a monopoly on serious personal problems.

So many troubled and curious teens came to hear his message that he moved from churches to large public auditoriums, both to accommodate the crowds and to attract the unchurched teen.

Because of this response Dave has spent most weekends since 1964 speaking to crowds all over the United States and Canada. When he toured England in 1966 the Beatles were playing in the same city. He outdrew them twice. A year later he drew similar crowds in Scandinavia, Belgium, Germany and France.

One of the reasons for these crowds is *The Cross and the Switchblade.* Many people just come to hear the author. Others come out of curiosity after seeing or hearing him interviewed on a local television or radio station. Numerous guest appearances make his schedule nerve-racking, but they keep the crusade costs very low.

The crowds that come don't hear fancy sermons. His messages are usually simple and catchy, like one entitled "Purple-Violet Squish," a hippie's psychedelic view of God.

His audience is mainly young people and he levels with them about their problems, such as how to handle parents, and sex. He

David Wilkerson speaks to a capacity crowd in the 6,200-seat Seattle Arena.
In Seattle and in many other cities teens flock to hear him talk about Teen Challenge, their hangups and how a personal relationship with Christ will fill the emptiness in their lives.

commented, "I don't harangue them with hell and judgment, because many are living in all kinds of hell now. I tell them Christ understands their problems and a personal relationship with Him will fill the gaps in their lives." At some point in the message — perhaps in the middle — Dave will close abruptly by saying, "If you want to straighten things out with God, come forward." No emotional mass appeal. Yet, hundreds come.

At a three-day crusade in Seattle over 1,300 pieces of literature were given out. Although only one piece of literature was given to each person who came to the counseling room there wasn't enough to go around. "The spiritual hunger was at a fever pitch," said Dave, who was making his third visit to Seattle. "About thirty percent of those who came forward were Roman Catholics. They were especially emotional."

Dave doesn't incite emotion, but still he doesn't forbid tears, as did one mother whose daughter had been crying on his shoulder after a meeting. The daughter, a frequent user of pot and about to have an illegitimate baby, was scolded, "Don't get all upset about religion." The next day this same mother became so blue over a soap opera on television that she couldn't fix supper. The girl wrote to Dave saying, "It doesn't make sense."

In the Seattle meetings many had problems worth crying about. Several girls were in love with married men. One was an unwed mother. Many had attempted or were considering suicide. Others whom Dave counseled complained of cold, dead churches, of ministers who didn't believe what they were preaching, of distrust of parents, sexual problems, and last and foremost, loneliness. "The majority that I speak with talk about loneliness," said Dave. "They have problems. They try to talk them out with their parents — but too often all they get is a five dollar bill and the sug-

"Man, I've been sitting here for fifteen minutes making fun of all these uneducated kids saying, 'This is all emotionalism.' But suddenly all my sins flashed in front of me and I saw myself for what I am and well . . . I need help."

Nineteen-year-old college student.

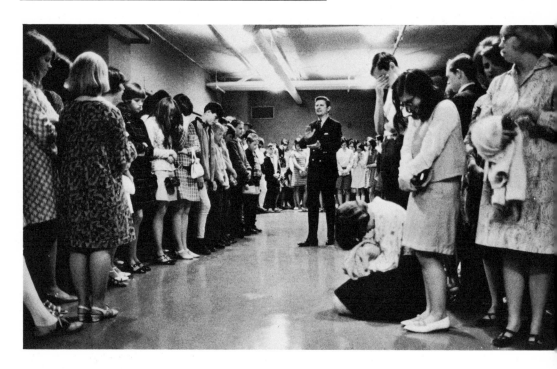

gestion, 'Go buy yourself something. See me when I'm not busy.' "

To help bridge this generation gap Dave often preaches the message "Why Kids Go Wrong" to the busy parents and rebellious teen-agers in the audience. Afterward, throughout the building there are usually many touching reunions between parents who realized their neglect and teens sorry for their bitterness and rebellion.

Many other teens who come forward for prayer and counseling find their problems no longer seem as large. One boy verbalized the new-found assurance evident on many faces. He said, "I'll still have problems, but now I'll be able to meet them. Now I've got Someone with me."

In the packed counseling room Dave talks to the group before introducing each member to a counselor.

112

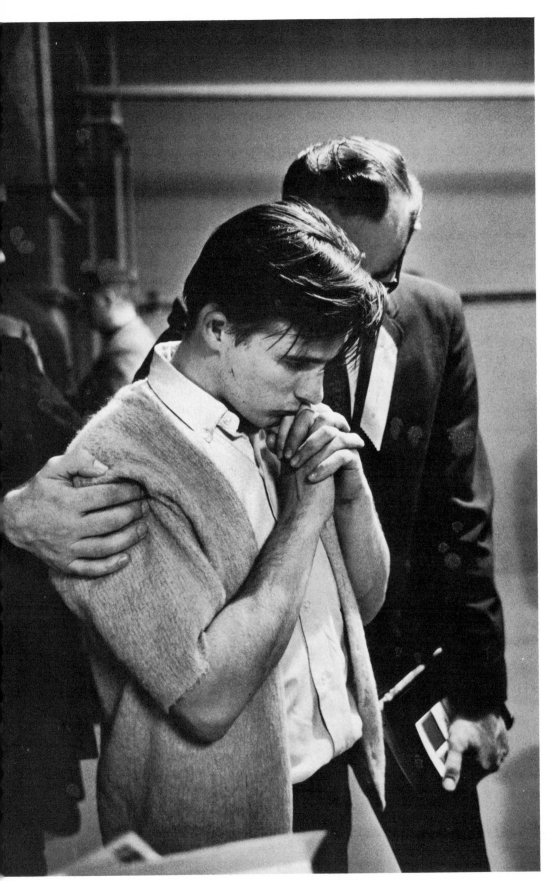

JOHNNY MELENDEZ

Fifteen-year-old Johnny Melendez lived in the middle of a battlefield.

His home was on 110th Street in Spanish Harlem, between Madison and Park Avenues, a block often called "the hottest block in Manhattan" because of the continual fighting and rumbling.

Johnny's army was the 107th street Dragons, the original Dragon gang. He had joined for the usual reasons: protection, excitement, parties and the gang's attractive "debs." Numbering about 300, it was a fairly large gang — and reportedly one of the toughest in New York. Combined with the many other independent Dragon divisions in Manhattan, Brooklyn, the Bronx and Queens, its strength was awesome.

Johnny realized just how big the Dragons were when several divisions scheduled a rumble with some Viceroys from Queens.

"Dragons from Brooklyn and the Lower East Side (Manhattan) came in stolen cars and three or four trucks," Johnny said. "Dragons from 96th Street rode bicycles. Then there were our allies, the Seminole Dragons, the Norsemen, the Daddies and the Sportsmen. I felt like I was just a number."

Perhaps 1000 packed Park Ave. between 116th and 120th Streets. On the rooftops they waited with shotguns, gasoline bombs and piles of bricks. In the hallways they waited with zip guns, switchblades, brass knuckles, garrison belts, chains and baseball bats.

Understandably, few residents had the

"I didn't care about anyone, including myself."

"When we weren't shooting anything else, we shot pool."

courage to leave their apartments, and, for several hours, Johnny didn't see a single policeman on the nearly deserted street. "They probably didn't dare to come until they got help from other precincts," he said.

The Viceroys never came. It's possible that they, too, were afraid — perhaps of the well-armed, well-entrenched Dragons — perhaps of being isolated in unfamiliar enemy territory with all routes of escape back to Queens blocked by the police.

Before Johnny joined the gang, he was a good student and the president of his eighth-grade class. Things were different in high school. When he did attend he often got into trouble — like the time he shoved a fellow student down a flight of stairs during an argument. After school he was jumped and stabbed by the other kid and three of his friends.

Johnny also got into trouble when he

skipped school. One day while playing hooky, Johnny and three friends decided to crash another high school for lunch. They shoved their way into line and stole a handful of meal tickets. Later they disrupted several classes and fought four students in a hallway until teachers broke it up. One friend, Sammy, fled during the fight; the four opponents disappeared afterward.

"We hung around in the school," said Johnny, "but when we got downstairs we saw three or four hundred guys, a huge mob, outside with sticks and bats waiting for us." The trio jumped a fence and ran to Franklin D. Roosevelt Drive, a nearby highway that runs up and down the east side of Manhattan.

"We began to run against the traffic," said Johnny. "Cars were swerving, screeching to a stop and honking, but we were more scared of all those guys behind us." They finally reached the Dragons and their home turf.

The turf is a gang's territory. Its invisible boundaries might extend only a few blocks but to the members of the gang it is sacred. Only on their turf are the members secure. A threat to the turf is a threat to each personally, and they will fight viciously to defend it. Young teen-agers have been known to stand up to even armed syndicate gangsters who jeopardized their turf.

Occasionally someone from a rival club will venture into enemy territory to discuss peace. When Sammy told Johnny and Pete, president of the Seminole Dragons, that Willie, a Viceroy, wanted to see them downstairs, they thought Willie wanted to settle the differences between the gangs. Willie's revolver told them they were wrong.

Another surprise was Willie's query to Sammy, "Should we burn (shoot) them?" Sammy, supposedly a Dragon, was actually a Viceroy spy. Willie had come to kill Johnny and Pete, but he hesitated. Dragons were playing ball outside. Others were listening to a juke box at the candy store across the street. If Willie pulled the trigger he would never get off Dragon turf alive. Willie pocketed the gun and, with Sammy, marched Pete and Johnny to the corner, where the two Viceroys hailed a cab and fled to their home turf.

Occasional rumbles and hit-and-run raids into enemy territory were dangerous, but

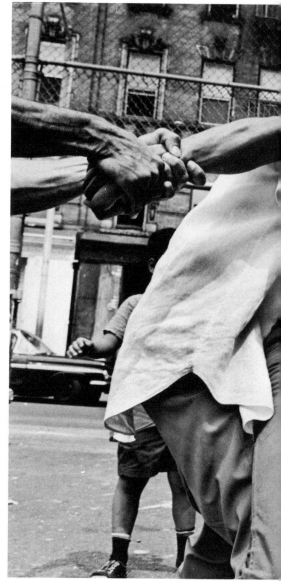

routine injuries were much more common. Johnny was badly burned when his zip gun exploded in his face. Like the others, he was continually being cut and bruised in such games as mock rumbles with lead-weighted garrison belts. Once he was stabbed after calling another Dragon "yellow." Of course, he wasn't always on the receiving end. One day on a dare he shot a friend in the leg.

His many wounds gave Johnny's mother reason to be worried about his safety. Finally she sent him to live with his father in Puerto Rico, Johnny's birthplace. The same day, his friend Pete was arrested and later imprisoned for carrying a pistol.

"In school I threw some
guy down the stairs.
After school his friends
jumped me and stabbed me."

"When pot loses its
kick, you want
something stronger."

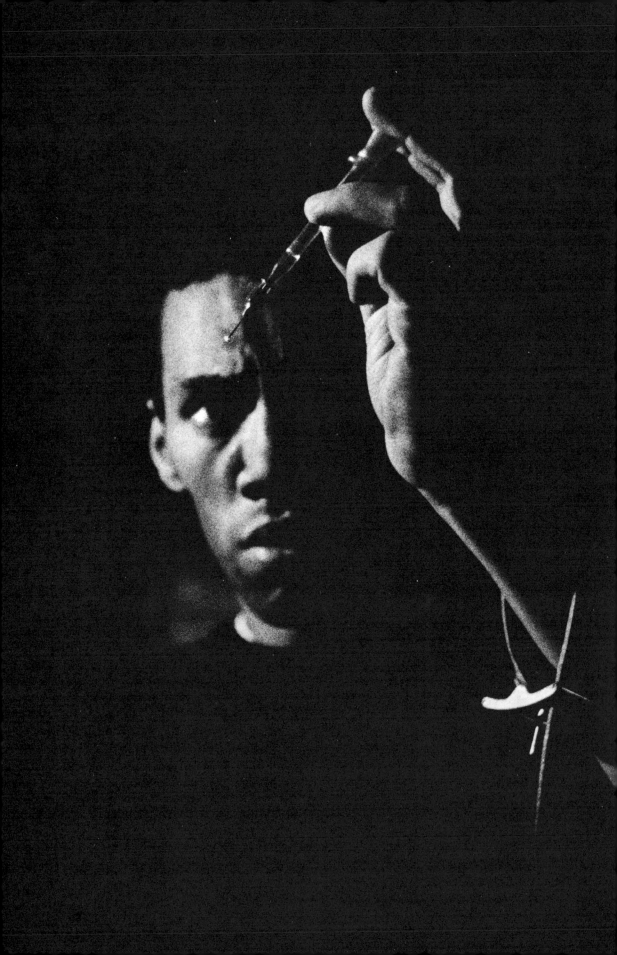

In Puerto Rico Johnny lied about his age (he was still only fifteen) and joined the National Guard. Less than a year later, after six months on active duty, he returned to New York and went to work for some Long Island City racketeers who distributed obscene magazines and lottery tickets. Gone were the levis, sweat shirts and switchblades. His new crowd dressed neat. Night clubs. Dancing. Marijuana. Liquor. Music.

Johnny played congo drums in a Spanish band. Another musician, an old friend who was once a Dragon, introduced Johnny to a new kick, something he never dreamed he'd try. In the back room of a night club his friend showed him how to inject heroin. The same night Johnny told himself, "I'm going to do this just on weekends when I go out dancing." Soon it was twice a week, three times, four.

After work he went with other addicts to rooftops, to basements, and to alleys to shoot dope. One night on a rooftop Johnny said casually, "You know, whenever I don't shoot dope I get a bad cold and a fever." His friend's answer startled him: "Baby, you're hooked!"

Other addicts gave Johnny the names of hospitals at which he could kick the habit. His first thought was, "I'll go, kick my dope habit, be well again, and then I'll use all the dope I want." In the next seven years he did try the hospitals. First, Manhattan State, then, Manhattan General, where he was given methadone. "That methadone — it's supposed to help you kick dope, but it gives you a habit, too. Man, it was worse than heroin because it wouldn't let me sleep. It drove me back to the streets to get a shot of dope."

Finally, a social worker persuaded Johnny to go to the federal hospital in Lexington, Kentucky. "There I met fellows imprisoned eight and nine years — K.Y. is also a prison. They told me the first thing they'd do when they got out was to get a shot of dope. I figured if they still weren't cured it was hopeless for me."

Released after several months, Johnny returned to New York. On his way back he said to himself, "I'm gonna get a job and start all over again. I'll go to night school to learn printing"; but before he was off the train in Penn Station the old craving for heroin returned. His first stop was to pawn his radio for a shot.

He also sought help from some friends who were involved in a type of spiritualism similar to voodoo. He knew they had some kind of power. At their dim, candle-lit meeting he was astounded to see a tiny, spirit-possessed lady, who thought she was a chicken, hopping around with a huge man on her shoulders while she cackled and furiously puffed a cigar.

When the little lady put the man down, the drums stopped. She called Johnny forward. "You have done many bad things," she told him. "You have not been caught. But time is short. Unless you listen to a good spirit you have within you, it will leave and you will die." She grabbed him and made hissing noises like a snake. Finally she gave him a complicated prescription, which included bathing at a beach at midnight three times during a full moon, and carrying three garlics in his pocket for a week.

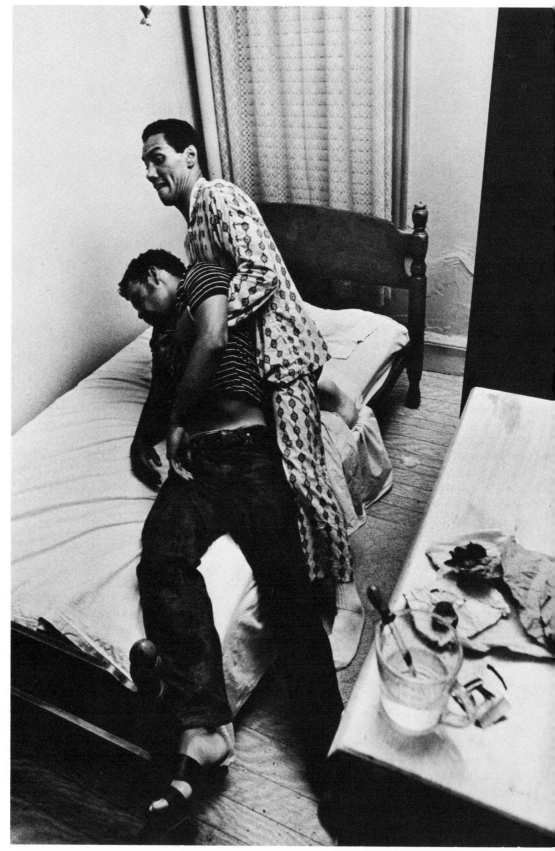

"A corpse in my room would be hard to explain."

Johnny left the service shaken but determined not to follow her advice. He knew
others who had. They had given the spiritualist a great deal of money and ended up looking "troubled, kind of crazy . . . like they
were possessed by something." He felt that
with spiritism, as with methadone, the cure
could be worse than the disease.

Unable to find an acceptable cure, he began to deliver heroin for syndicate distributors. More frequently, he would steal and
sell heroin himself. Early one morning he almost had a dead customer to dispose of.
Tarzan, Johnny's best friend, stopped by his
room. Tarzan bought three bags and pro-
ceeded to inject them.

"You sure you can take that much?"
Johnny asked.

"Yeah. It's O.K."

Tarzan shot the heroin and almost immediately passed out. He had taken an overdose. Johnny frantically dragged Tarzan onto
the bed. A corpse in his room would be hard
to explain; besides, Tarzan was his friend.

Grabbing the needle, Johnny filled it with
salt water and injected it into Tarzan's arm.
Next he tried to force some milk down Tarzan's throat (milk supposedly neutralizes the
effect of heroin). He was interrupted by a
knock at the door. Danny, who had come to
beg for a bag of heroin, took one look at the
milk-soaked body and said, "I'll see you
around, Johnny." Fortunately for Tarzan,
Johnny stayed and eventually revived him.

His mother feared Johnny would die of an
overdose or a policeman's bullet, as had
many of his friends. He later said, "My mother
cried many times at night. She didn't sleep
very much because I'm her only son. When I
lived at home she used to watch for me all
the time out of the window."

Perhaps two dozen times he tried to kick
his habit at home. During one of these times
he became so sick that, in spite of his mother's pleas, he stumbled out of the apartment
and down the street to wait for the connection. It was cold outside, so Johnny went into
a bakery for a cup of coffee. Inside, another
addict was showing a Teen Challenge card
to a girl. Neither wanted the card, so Johnny
took it.

The pusher never came. When Johnny returned to his mother's, she was still crying.
Again she told him that he would die if he

"My mother cried many times."

"Nicky Cruz answered my call for help."

didn't stop. He showed her the card he had been given, and she begged him to phone Teen Challenge.

Reluctantly, he called. Nicky Cruz answered. Nicky was a former leader of the Brooklyn Mau Maus, and at that time, Evangelism Director of Teen Challenge. He listened to Johnny's story and agreed to meet Johnny that night on East 125th Street in Harlem.

Johnny was shivering when Nicky met him. He had on a thin jacket and he was beginning to have chills from withdrawal. Nicky threw his own coat over Johnny's shoulders and helped him to the truck. When they arrived at Teen Challenge in Brooklyn, Johnny was surprised to see many of his old friends, some who had shot drugs with him, some who were gang members. They crowded around, telling him how Christ had cleaned them up; but Johnny couldn't understand because everyone was speaking at once. And he was sick and becoming sicker.

Nicky took him into the office and began to tell him about God and Jesus Christ. Johnny interrupted, "I've got my own philosophy about Christ. I used to see big signs in the subway saying 'Christ died for our sins.' If He did, I figure I can sin all I want." Nicky showed him in the Bible that he was wrong. Then he told Johnny to kneel down to pray.

"He was praying real loud and it bothered me," Johnny said later. "I wasn't used to it.

He was saying, 'God, take away the desire for drugs, the desire for marijuana, the desire for liquor,' and things like that. I was there doing nothing and I was getting sicker because I couldn't get a shot of dope that night.

"Then he grabbed me by the arm and said, 'Johnny, if you really want help, you have to ask God yourself. You have to ask God to change your life and take away your habits.'

"I began to remember my grandmother in Puerto Rico. She used to take me to a Catholic church when I was very young. I was real scared of the big statue of Christ on the cross with His side bleeding and thorns on His head. She would try to get me to come near it to kiss its feet but I'd say, 'No good. I'm not going up there.'

"One morning she persuaded me to go up saying, 'He's not going to hurt you. He's good,' and she told me about Him. After that I always liked that statue.

"I began to remember all this when I was there with Nicky. Then something I didn't know I had within me began to cry out to God. It wasn't a beautiful prayer. I simply asked God to come into me and to give me a completely new life.

"As I was praying, it seemed that there was something going on within me. I'd been sick and was getting real bad, but when I got up my withdrawal pains had left me and I was feeling real good; there was nothing wrong with me."

The next day Johnny went to Prospect Park to play ball with the others. Nicky came over and threw his arms around Johnny. "Did the Lord do something for you last night, Johnny?" he asked.

Johnny replied, "Man, He sure did, or else I wouldn't be with you guys out here." It usually took him two weeks to withdraw.

Then began the mental battle. Johnny could not shake the thought, "You're all right now. Leave the center, make new friends, and earn money by playing congo drums in the band. You don't have to shoot dope." Every time Nicky or the other boys saw Johnny with a faraway look in his eyes — sometimes three or four times a day — they took him into the chapel and prayed for him. He wisely heeded their advice. He stayed.

After only two weeks at the center, he went to the farm in Rehrersburg. Gradually he began to think more about his classes and God, and less about earning money with the band. Several months later he began to fear going home. The fellows would ask him, "When are you going to New York City?" and he would reply, "Never mind. I don't want to go back for a long time, until I'm sure I'm not going to do the same thing again. I want to forget the city and concentrate on getting my mind cleared up." Six months after entering the program he went on his first pass.

When Johnny was dealing heroin, he was always relaxed. He had frequently encountered detectives while carrying thirty to forty bags of heroin, but he was always so calm and friendly they never thought to search him; however, coming through the Lincoln Tunnel on his first pass, he became very shaky.

"I began to send up SOS's to heaven real quick," he said later. "I knew what I'd find in New York City: marijuana, dope, and everything." The first thing he did was go into the chapel at the Teen Challenge center. He finally ventured forth, but he returned to the chapel frequently while on his pass.

The reactions of his old friends varied. Some, who called him "hoodlum priest," "fanatic" and "hallelujah," thought he was only after girls in the church. Others were impressed. The Spiritualist who had tried to help him said, "You look different than before. You look like you're full of life."

"Through Nicky I found help in God."

Months later, Johnny spoke at a Teen Challenge street meeting near his home in Spanish Harlem. After he finished telling the many addicts who had gathered what God had done for him, a sixteen-year-old boy shook his hand, and with tears in his eyes, said, "Johnny, you don't know how happy I feel to see you doing this."

Johnny had often gotten high on pot and taken that boy onto a rooftop to play his congo drums. "Now," Johnny said, "someone who had taught him to play drums was showing him something worthwhile, something he would never forget. That really touched me."

Johnny finished the rehabilitation program, and in September, 1965, enrolled at Northeast Bible College in Pennsylvania. Two years later, he dropped out for a year to complete high school by mail. In September, 1968, he resumed his studies at Southwestern Bible College in Waxahachie, Texas. Upon graduation Johnny would like to attend seminary for a year or two.

His goal is to organize churches in remote sections of Latin America. "I'd like to stay in one place two or three years to help build a church, organize the Christians, and teach them until good men are raised up to take over."

"At one time I didn't care about anyone, even myself," Johnny has said. Today his life is dedicated to serving others and God.

"Some of my friends called me a 'hoodlum priest' but some listened."

"There is a spot at the farm where I liked to be alone, read my Bible and pray."

"I quit Bible school for a year to get my high-school diploma."

"I taught a Spanish class at the center when I got out of the farm and during vacations since then. Eventually I want to go to Latin America to organize churches and teach until good men are raised up. Then I'll start all over."

127

"Love is not only something you feel. It's something you do."

Rev. David Wilkerson

TEEN CHALLENGE
444 CLINTON AVE.
BROOKLYN, N.Y.
11238